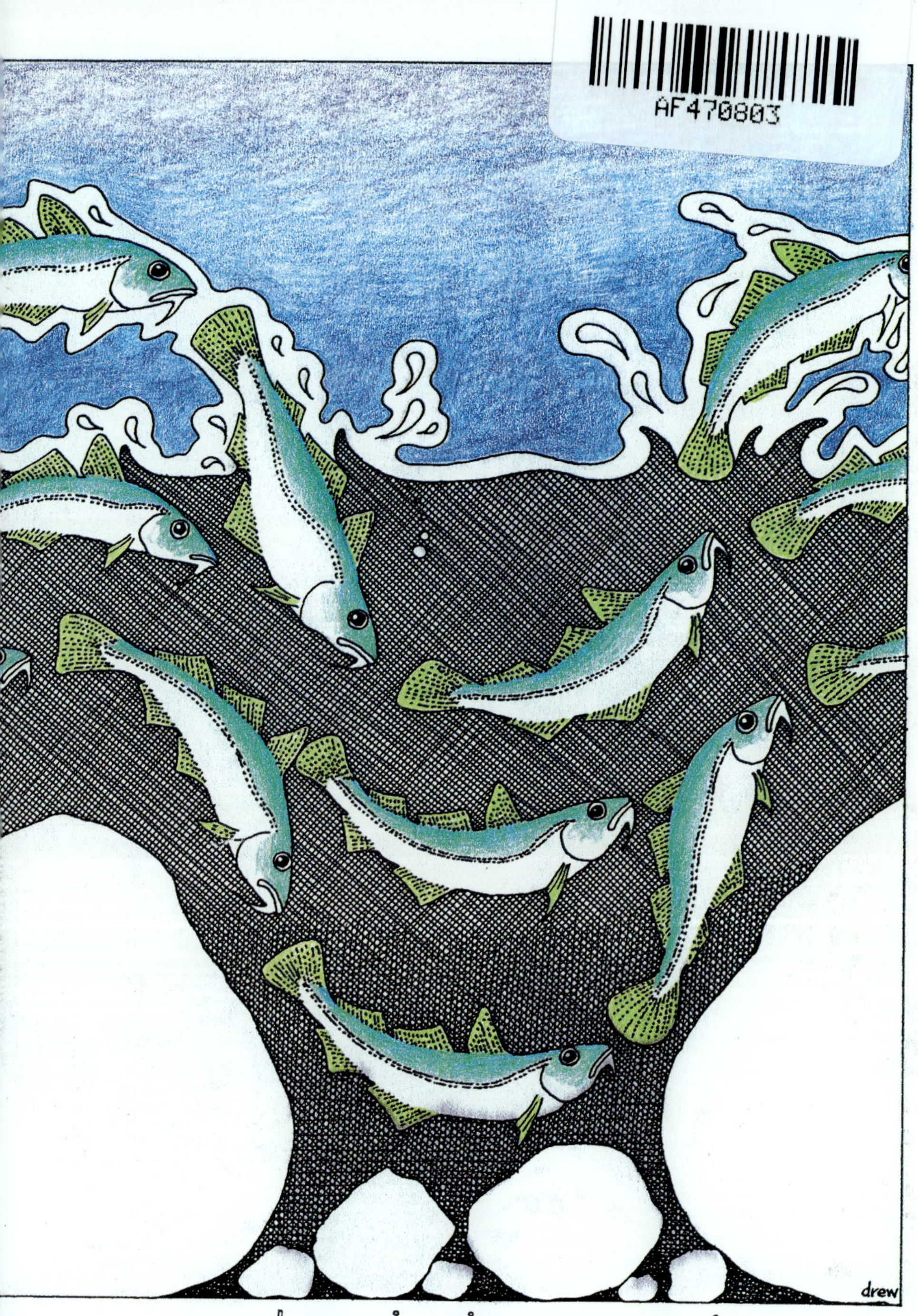

cod moving in a mysterious way

SIMON DREW'S

BEASTLY
BIRTHDAY BOOK

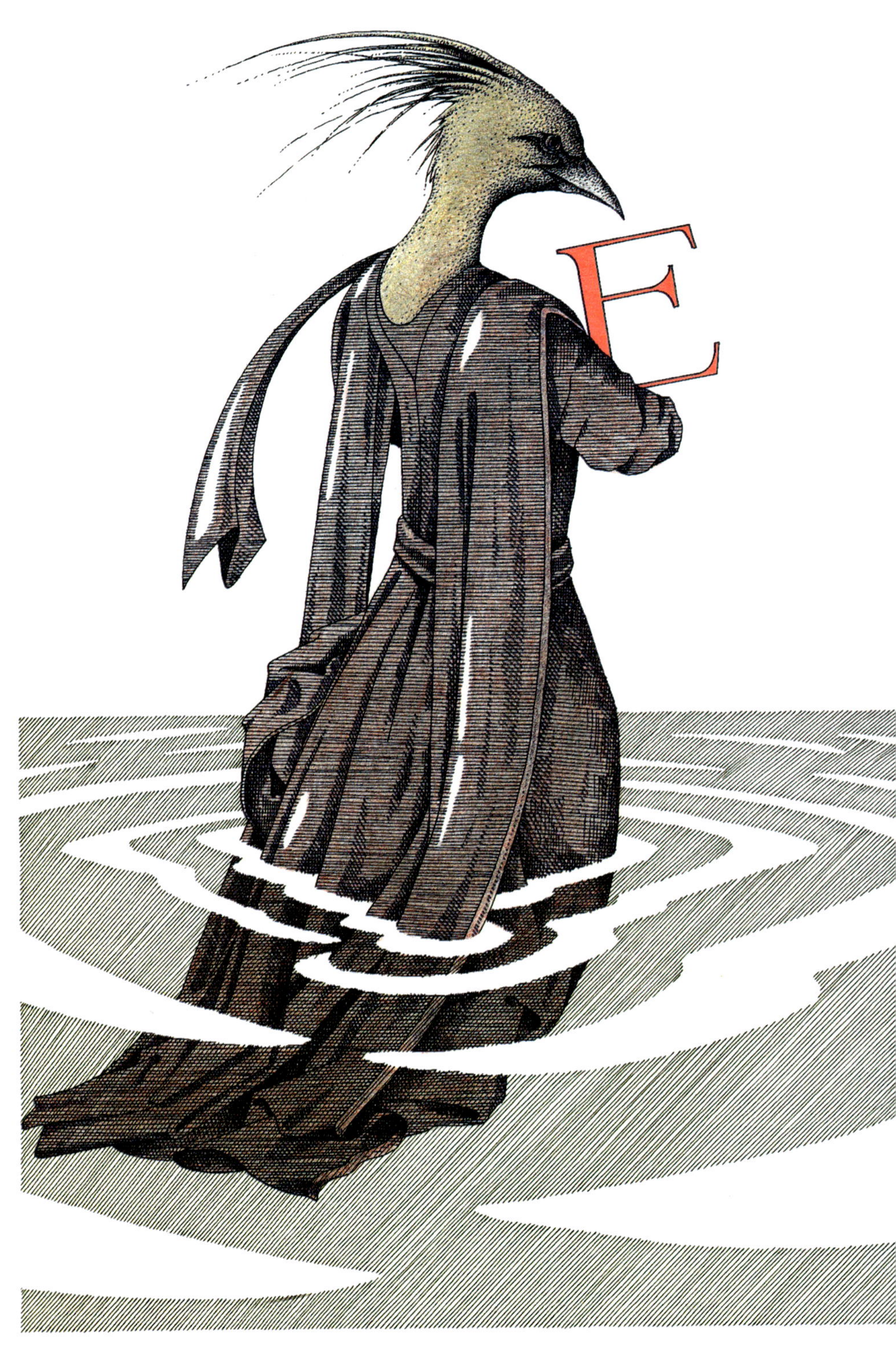
E

SIMON DREW'S
BEASTLY
BIRTHDAY BOOK

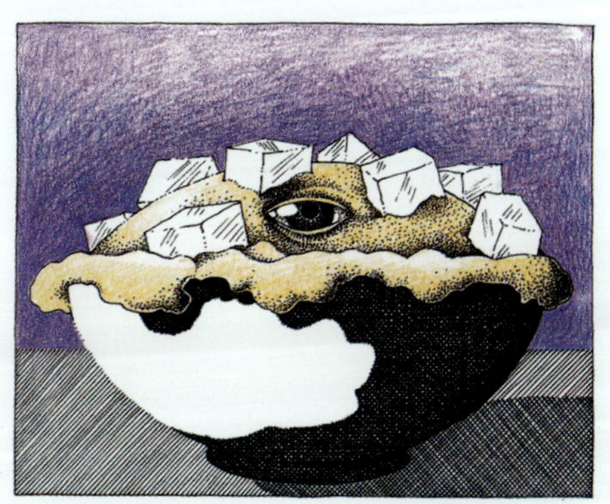

Ice pie (with my little eye)

ANTIQUE COLLECTORS CLUB

© 1995 Simon Drew
World copyright reserved

ISBN 1 85149 220 8

British Library Cataloguing in Publication Data
A catalogue record for this book is available from the British Library

Printed in England by the Antique Collectors' Club Ltd., Woodbridge, Suffolk IP12 1DS
on Consort Royal Satin paper from Donside Mills, Aberdeen

THE INTRODUCTION

This is a book for looking
at the future.

Here are two important
quotations that have always
acted as guides for me:

Oscar Wilde: "Anything worth
learning cannot be taught."

McLandburgh Wilson:
"Twixt the optimist and the pessimist
The difference is droll:
The optimist sees the doughnut
But the pessimist sees the hole."

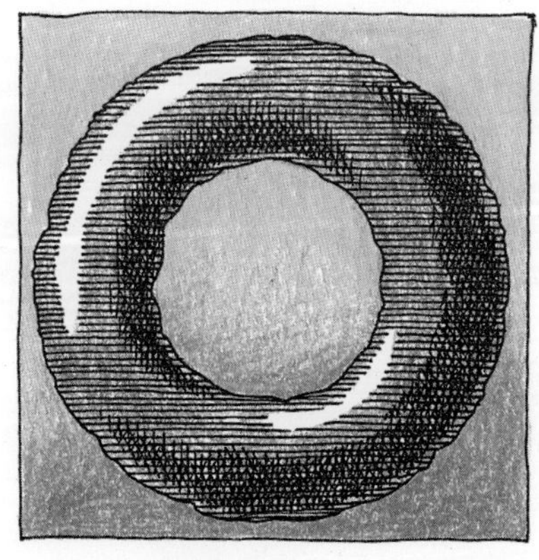

fig. 1

CAPRICORN
(the goat) dec 22 to jan 19

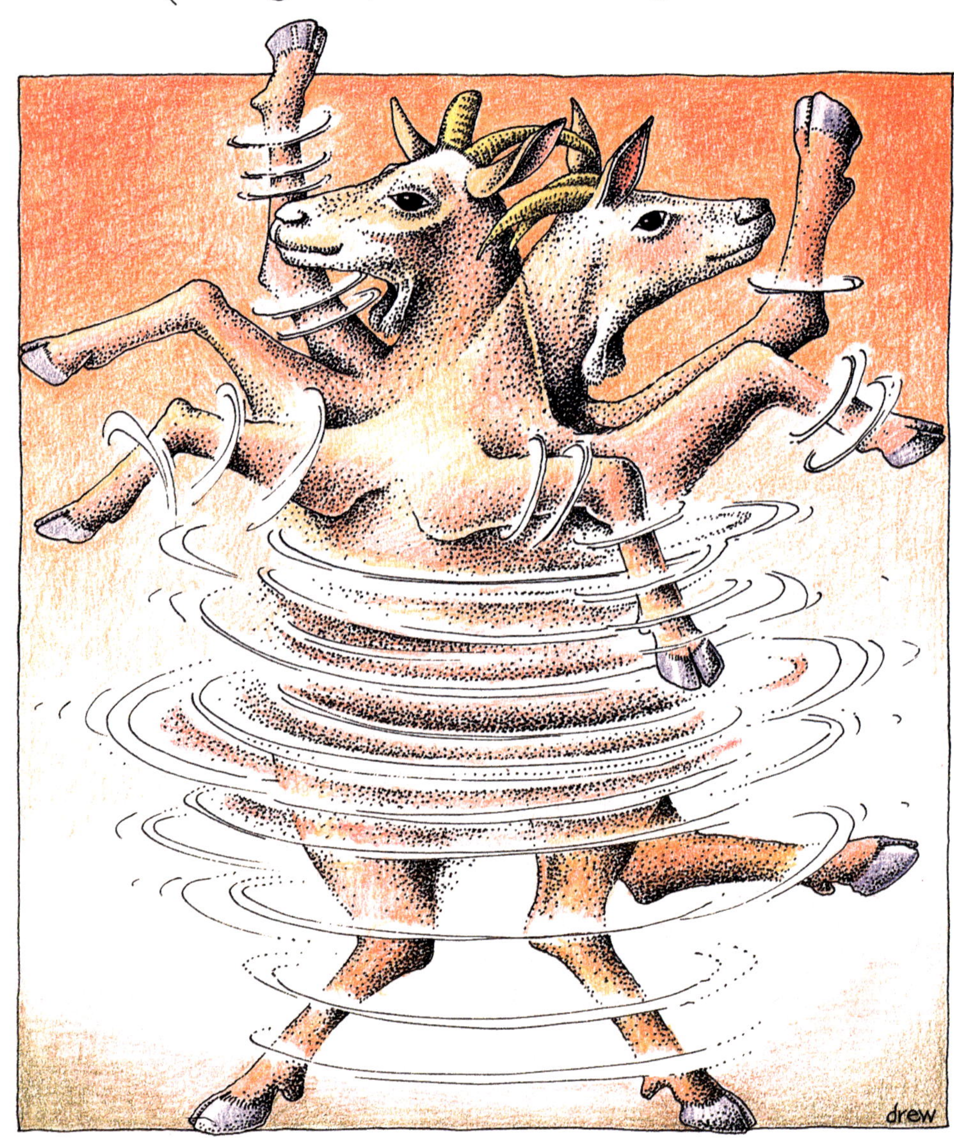

acting the giddy goat
(also known as: a goat of arms)

CAPRICORN

Those who are born underneath this great sign
are thoughtful, successful and certain to shine,
and help blind old ladies when crossing the road,
and kiss every frog but avoid every toad.
   Their greatest ambition, though not so
                                    well known
is finding a bank that will give them a loan.
They roll up one trouser leg when it looks fine
and never refuse any offer of wine.

dec 22

christmas carol day

dec 23

stonemason day

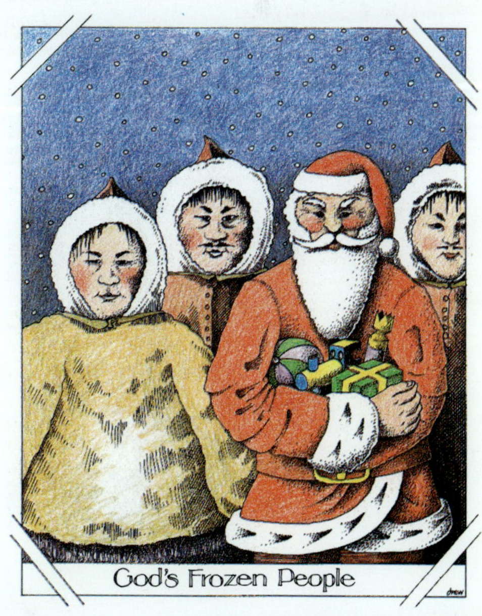

God's Frozen People

dec 24

dollar day

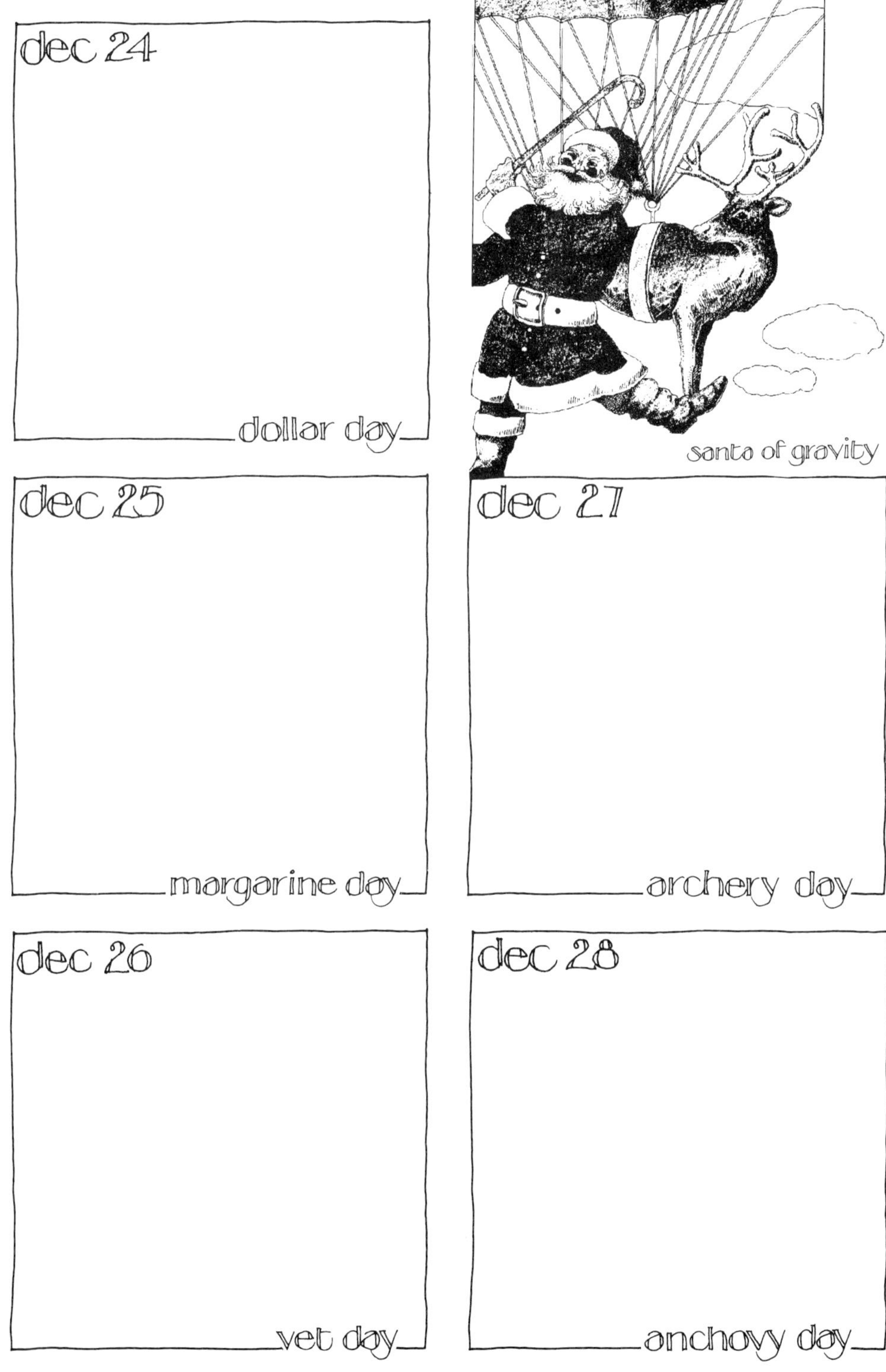

santa of gravity

dec 25

margarine day

dec 27

archery day

dec 26

vet day

dec 28

anchovy day

<table>
<tr><td>

dec 29

ostrich day
</td><td>

jan 1

trouser day
</td></tr>
<tr><td>

dec 30

blizzard day
</td><td>

jan 2

snorkel day
</td></tr>
<tr><td>

dec 31

end-of-the day
</td><td>

jan 3

pincushion day
</td></tr>
</table>

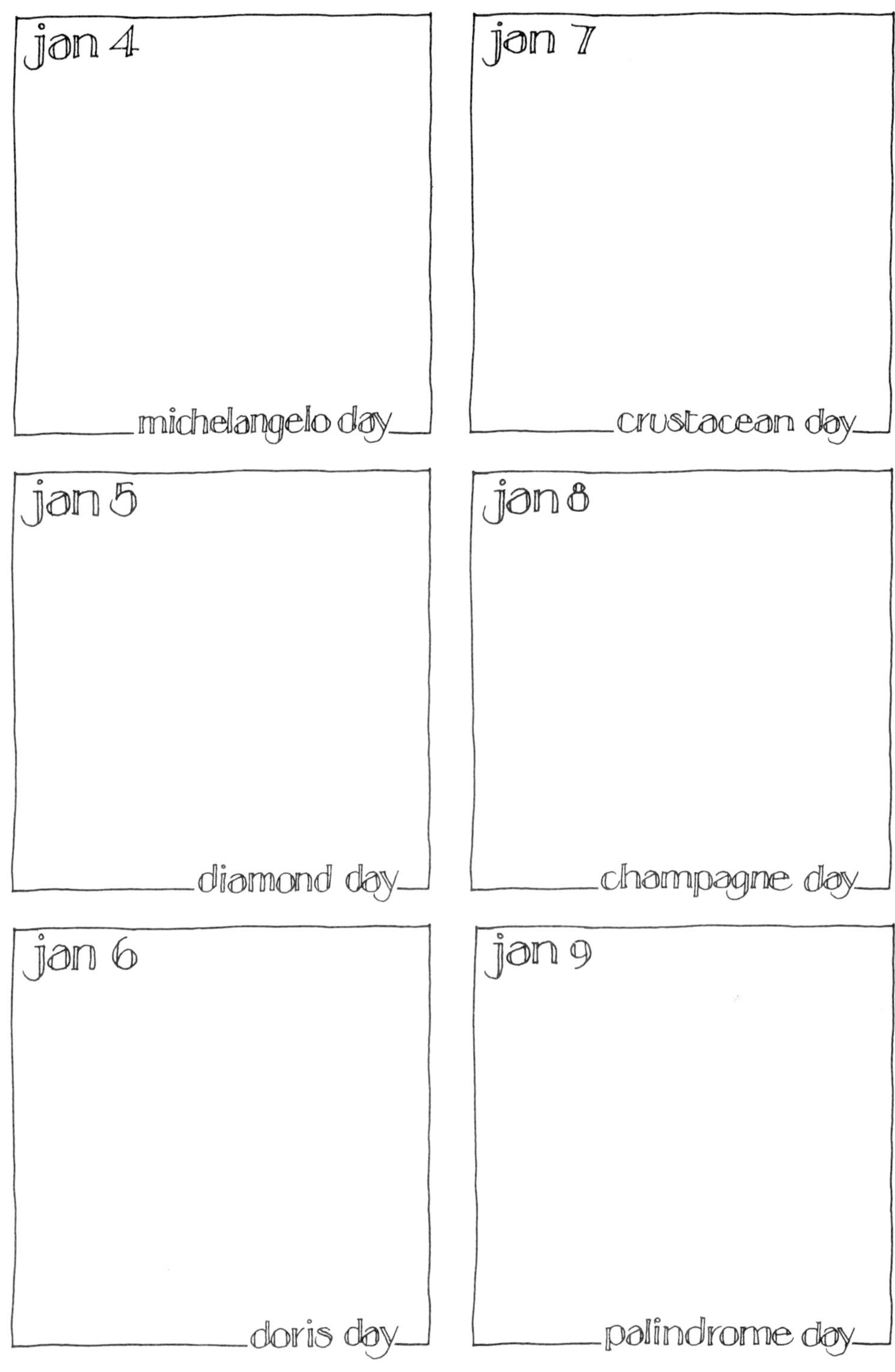

jan 4
michelangelo day
jan 7
crustacean day
jan 5
diamond day
jan 8
champagne day
jan 6
doris day
jan 9
palindrome day

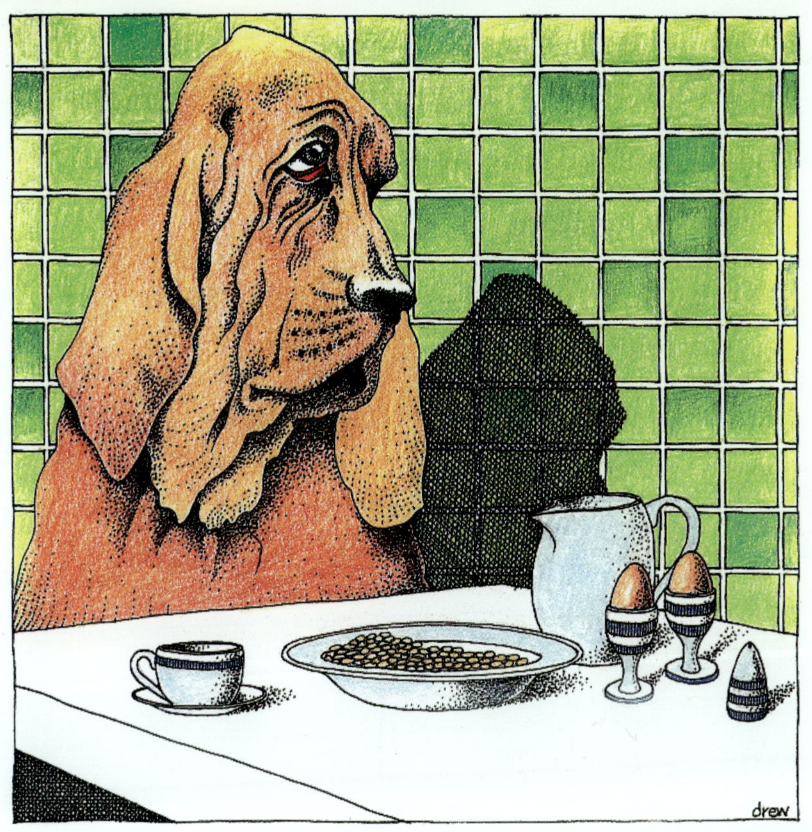

only dull people
are bright at breakfast.

jan 10

jan 11

chocolate button day

parsnip day

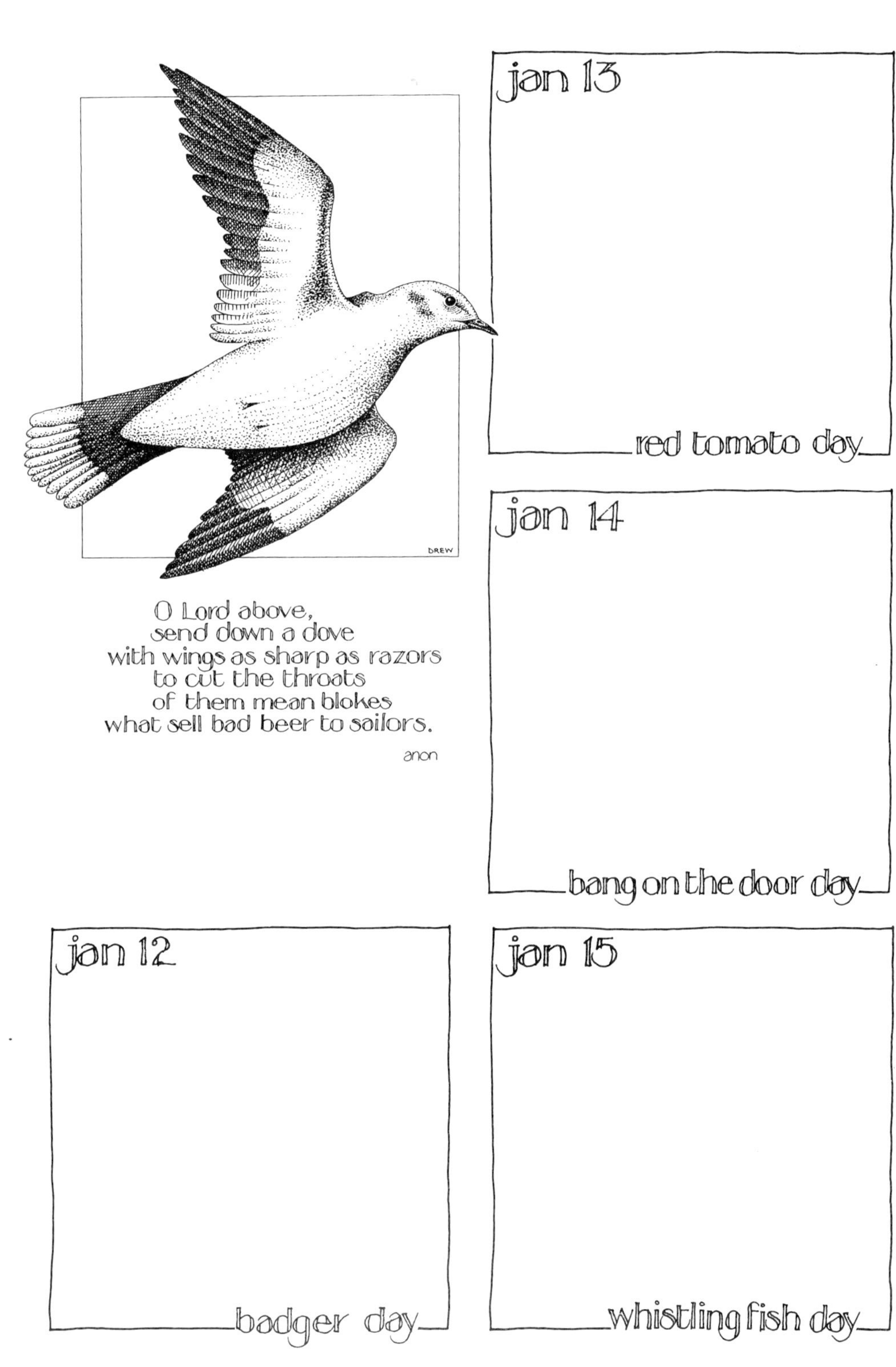
DREW

O Lord above,
send down a dove
with wings as sharp as razors
to cut the throats
of them mean blokes
what sell bad beer to sailors.

anon

jan 13

red tomato day

jan 14

bang on the door day

jan 12

badger day

jan 15

whistling fish day

jan 16

hiccough day

jan 18

sofa day

jan 17

dog day

jan 19

zipperdeedoodah day

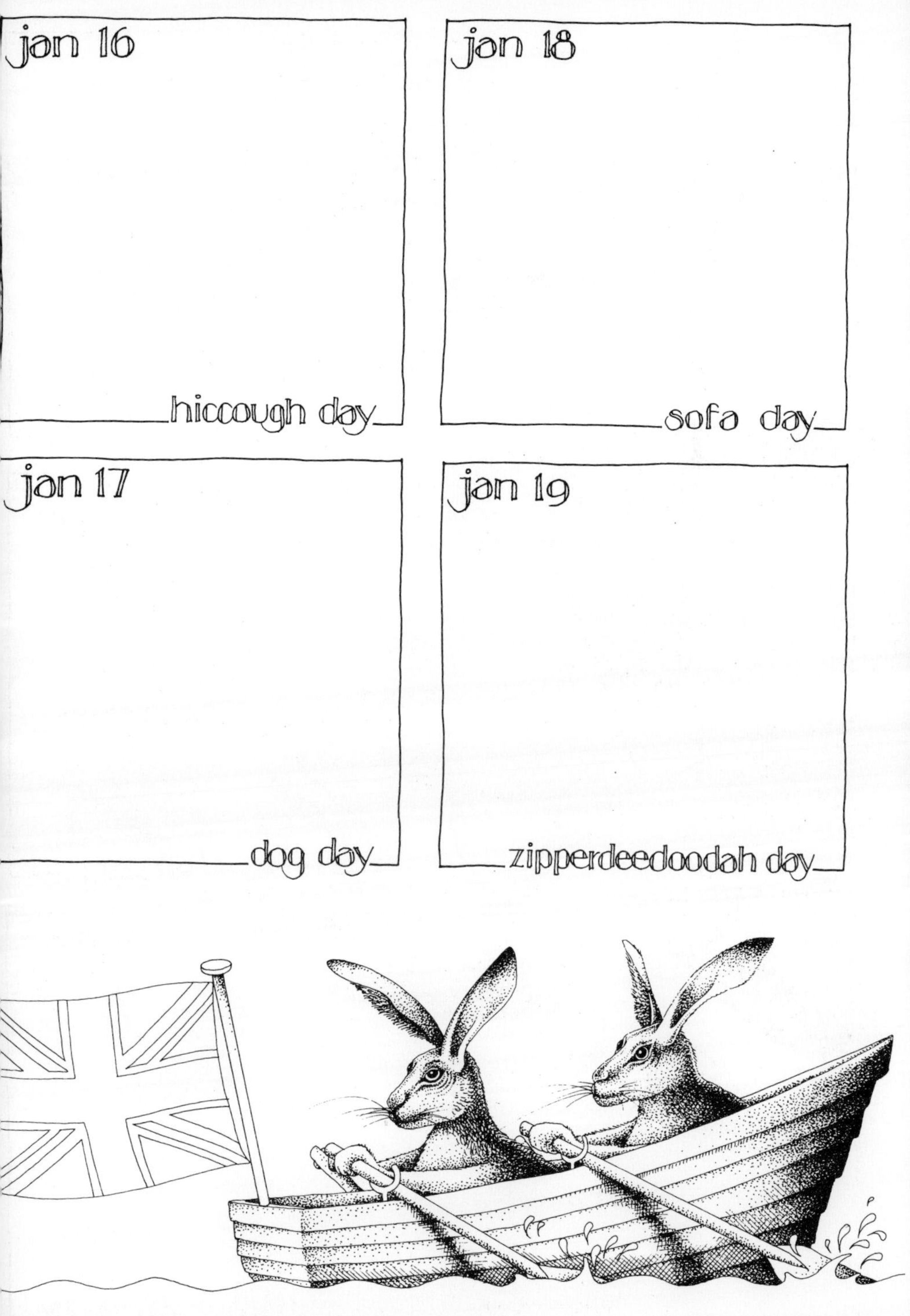

AQUARIUS
(the waterbearer) jan 20 to feb 18

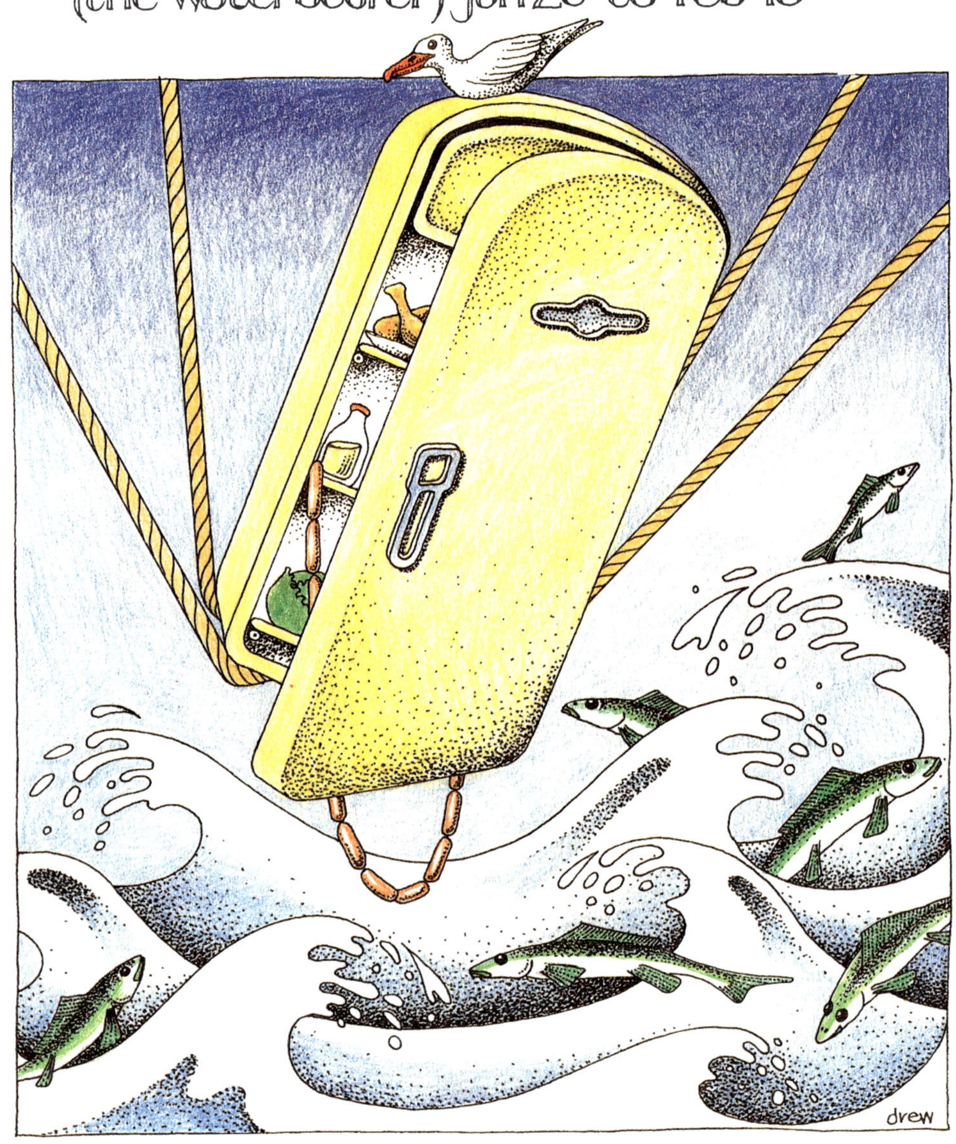

fridge
over troubled water

AQUARIUS

Those who are born underneath this great sign
are thoughtful, successful and certain to shine.
They're made slightly nervous when given a snake.
They've never been known to admit a mistake,
but give them a reason to help a lost soul
they tackle the problem and swallow it whole:
and when it is solved they will hurry away
and no one will know of the hero that day.

jan 20

nostril day

jan 21

beetroot day

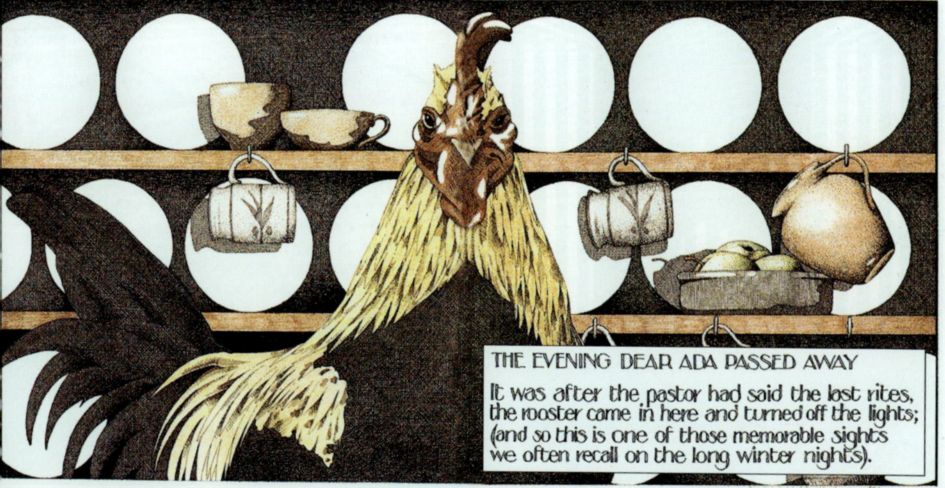

THE EVENING DEAR ADA PASSED AWAY

It was after the pastor had said the last rites,
the rooster came in here and turned off the lights;
(and so this is one of those memorable sights
we often recall on the long winter nights).

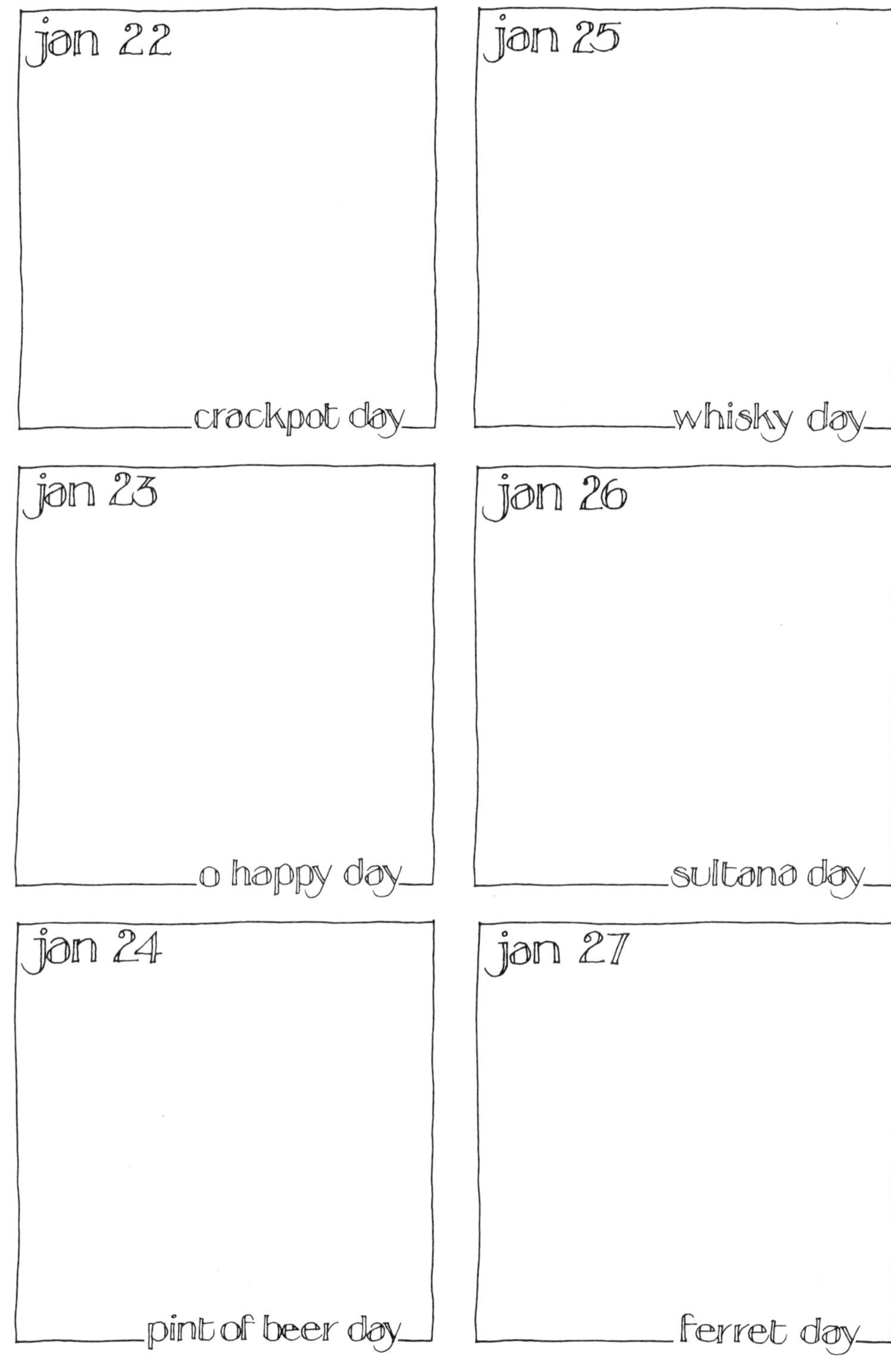

jan 22
crackpot day
jan 23
o happy day
jan 24
pint of beer day
jan 25
whisky day
jan 26
sultana day
jan 27
ferret day

jan 28

_______octopus day_

jan 29

_______soap dish day_

jan 30

_______pencil day_

jan 31

_______plastic duck day_

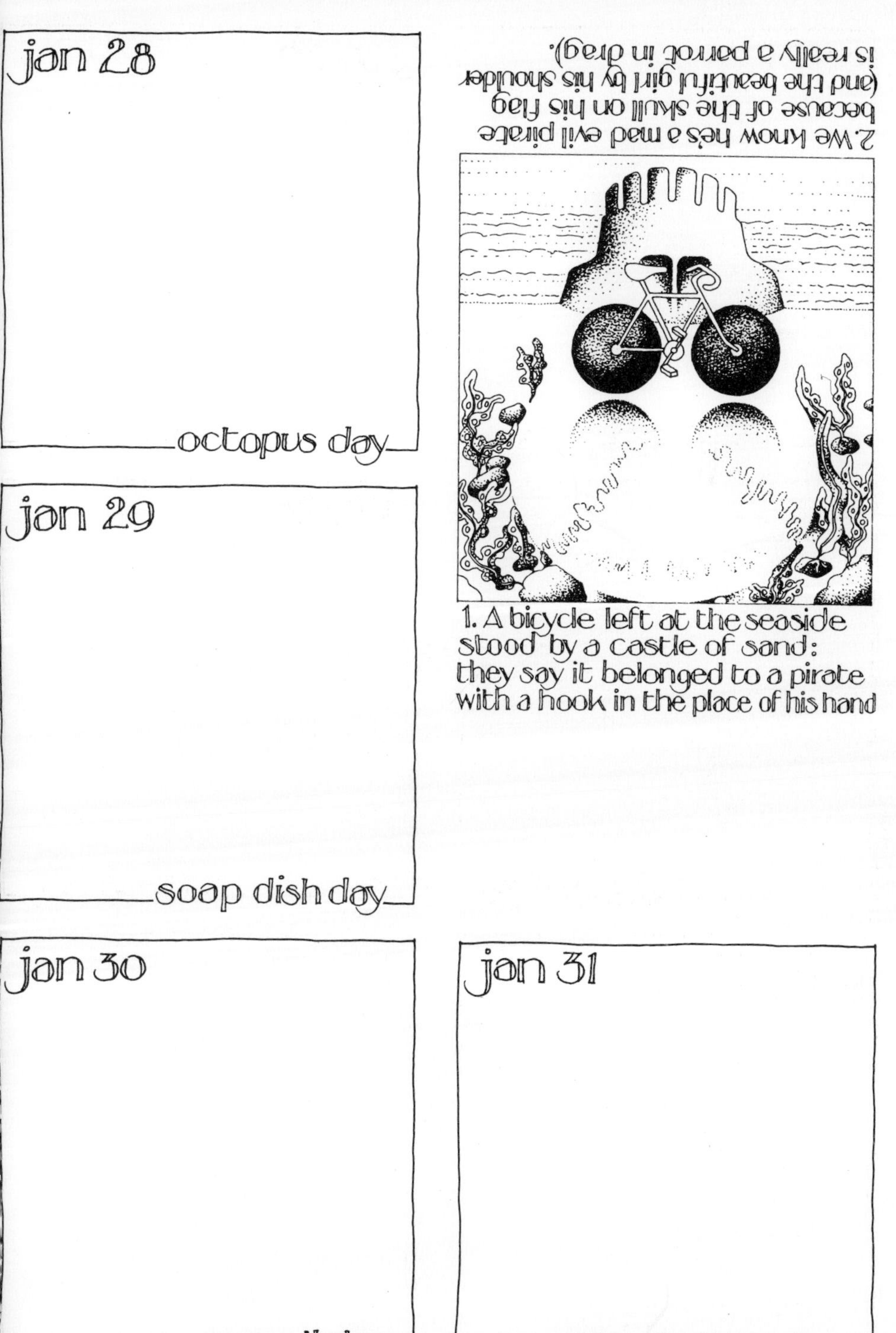

2. We know he's a mad evil pirate
because of the skull on his flag
(and the beautiful girl by his shoulder
is really a parrot in drag).

1. A bicycle left at the seaside
stood by a castle of sand:
they say it belonged to a pirate
with a hook in the place of his hand

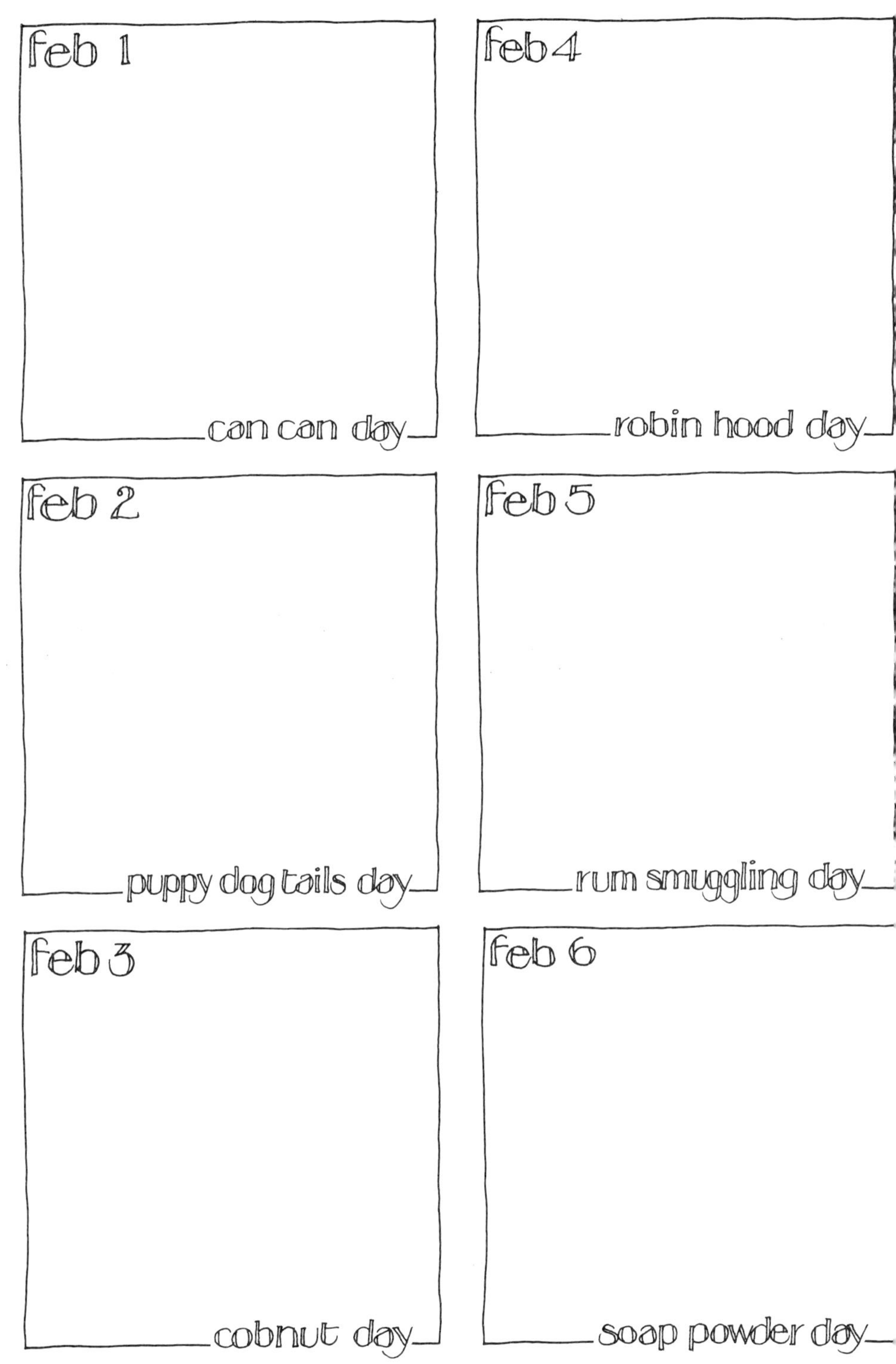

feb 1
can can day

feb 4
robin hood day

feb 2
puppy dog tails day

feb 5
rum smuggling day

feb 3
cobnut day

feb 6
soap powder day

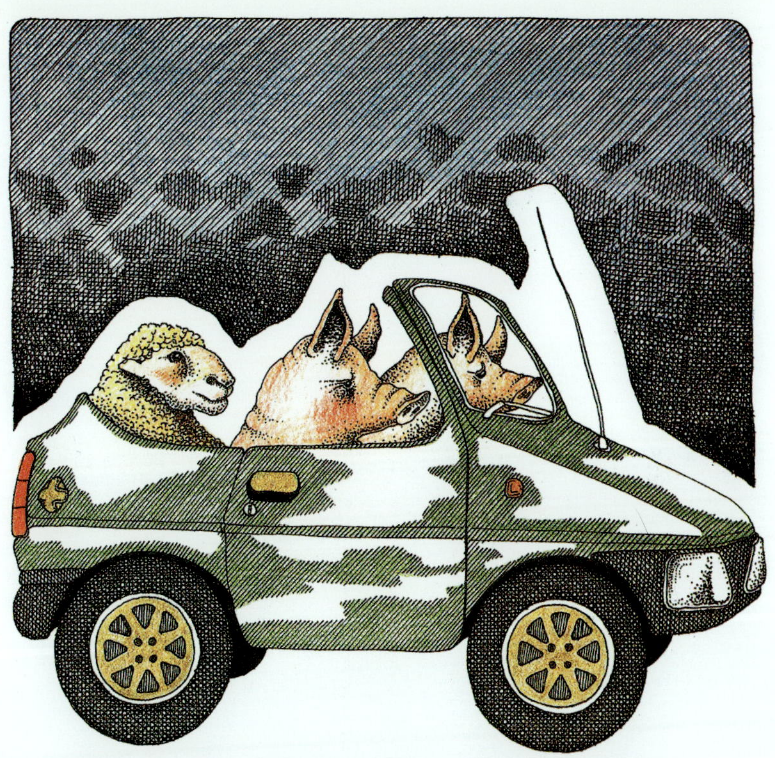

the truth about the road hog
however hard you hunt,
if pigs are in the front....
I'll bet you a fiver
there's a back sheep driver.

feb 7	feb 8
cheddar day	sandbags day

feb 9

___ OK day___

feb 11

___ gravy day___

feb 10

___ tea leaf day___

feb 12

___ big decision day___

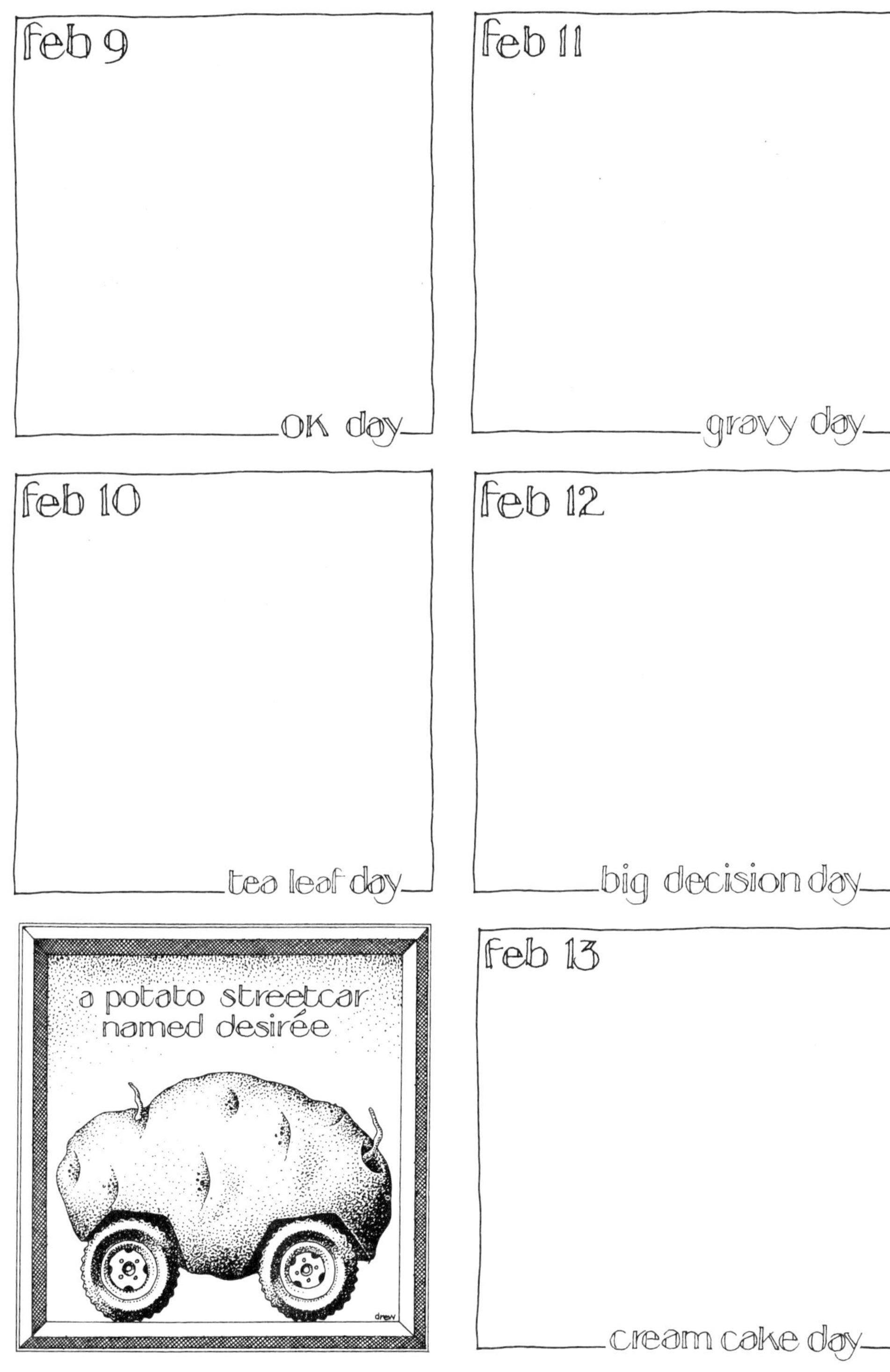

feb 13

___ cream cake day___

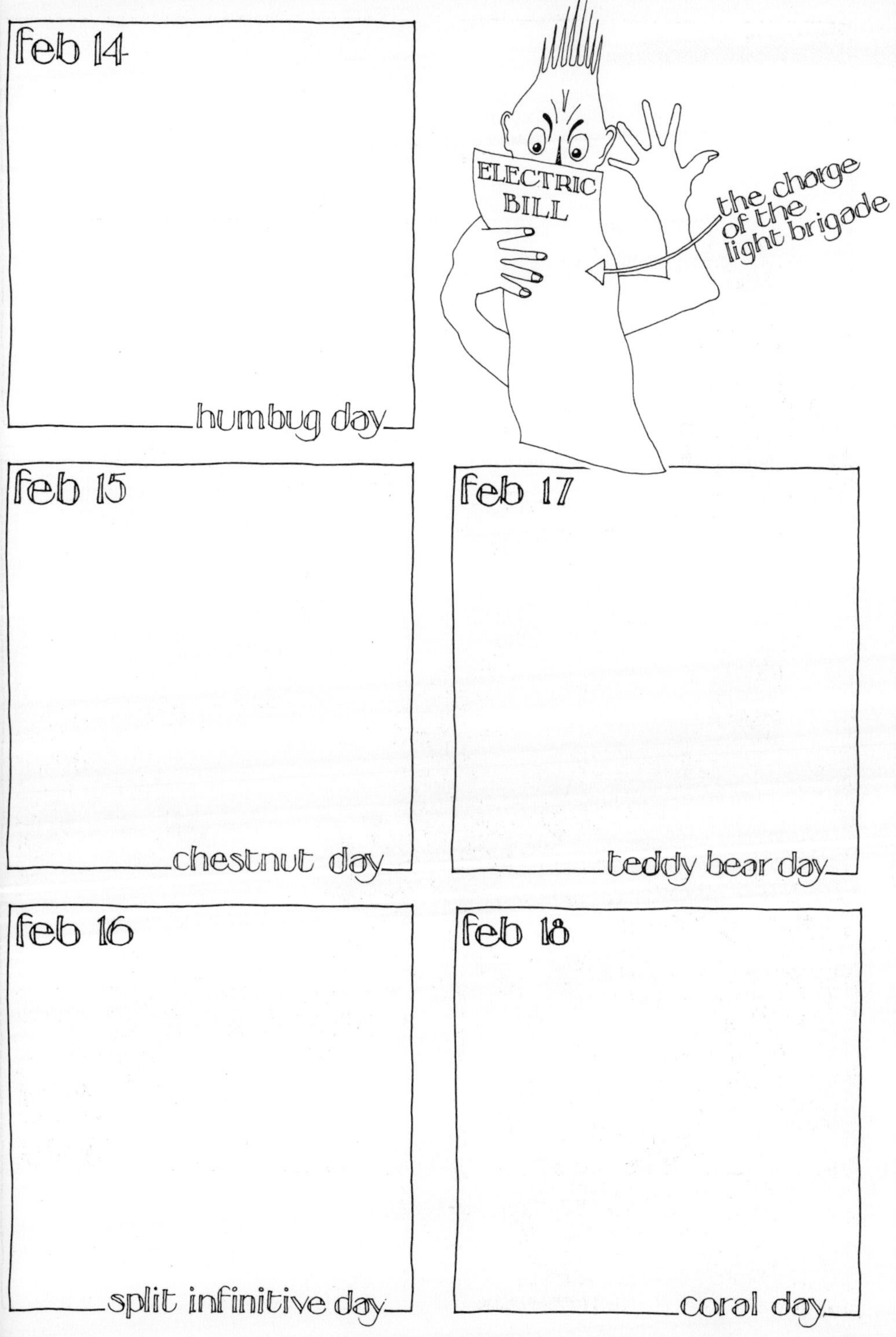

feb 14

_______humbug day_

feb 15

_____chestnut day_

feb 16

___split infinitive day_

feb 17

_____teddy bear day_

feb 18

_____coral day_

PISCES
(the fishes) feb 19 to mar 20

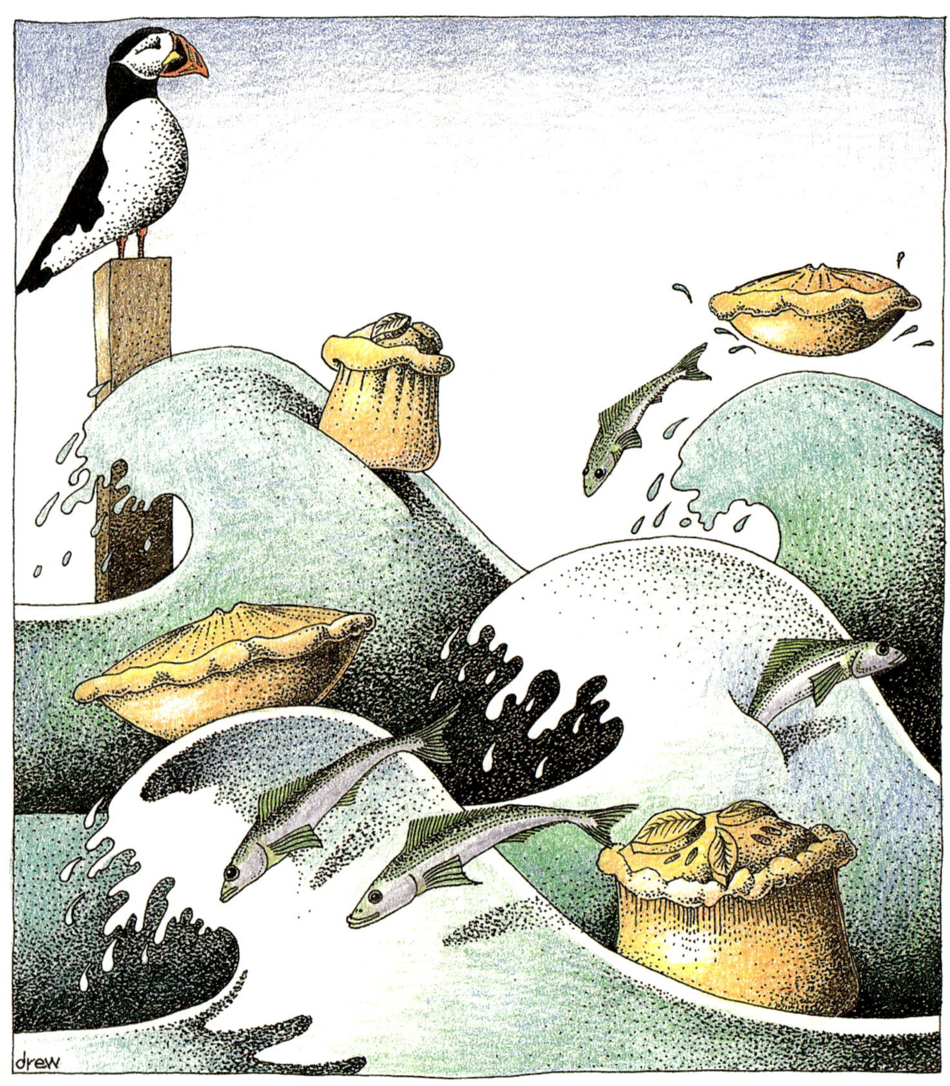

pie
seas

PISCES
Those who are born underneath this great sign
are thoughtful, successful and certain to shine.
They have this desire to plan out the world:
whenever hair's straight, they soon want it
curled.

Find them a house that is memory-filled,
they'd rather demolish, design and rebuild;
give them an item of perfect design
there'll always be something they want to
refine.

feb 19

giraffe day

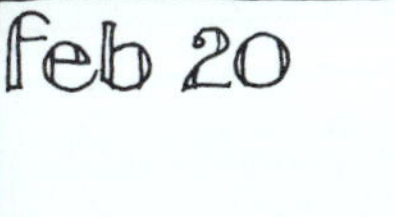

feb 20

pork pie day

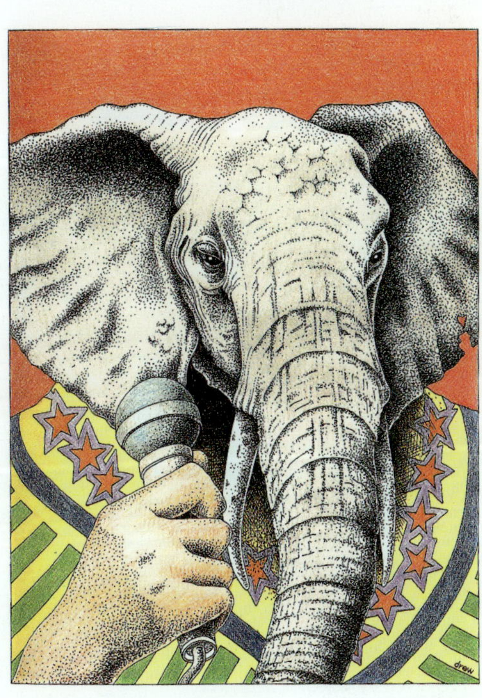

elephants gerald

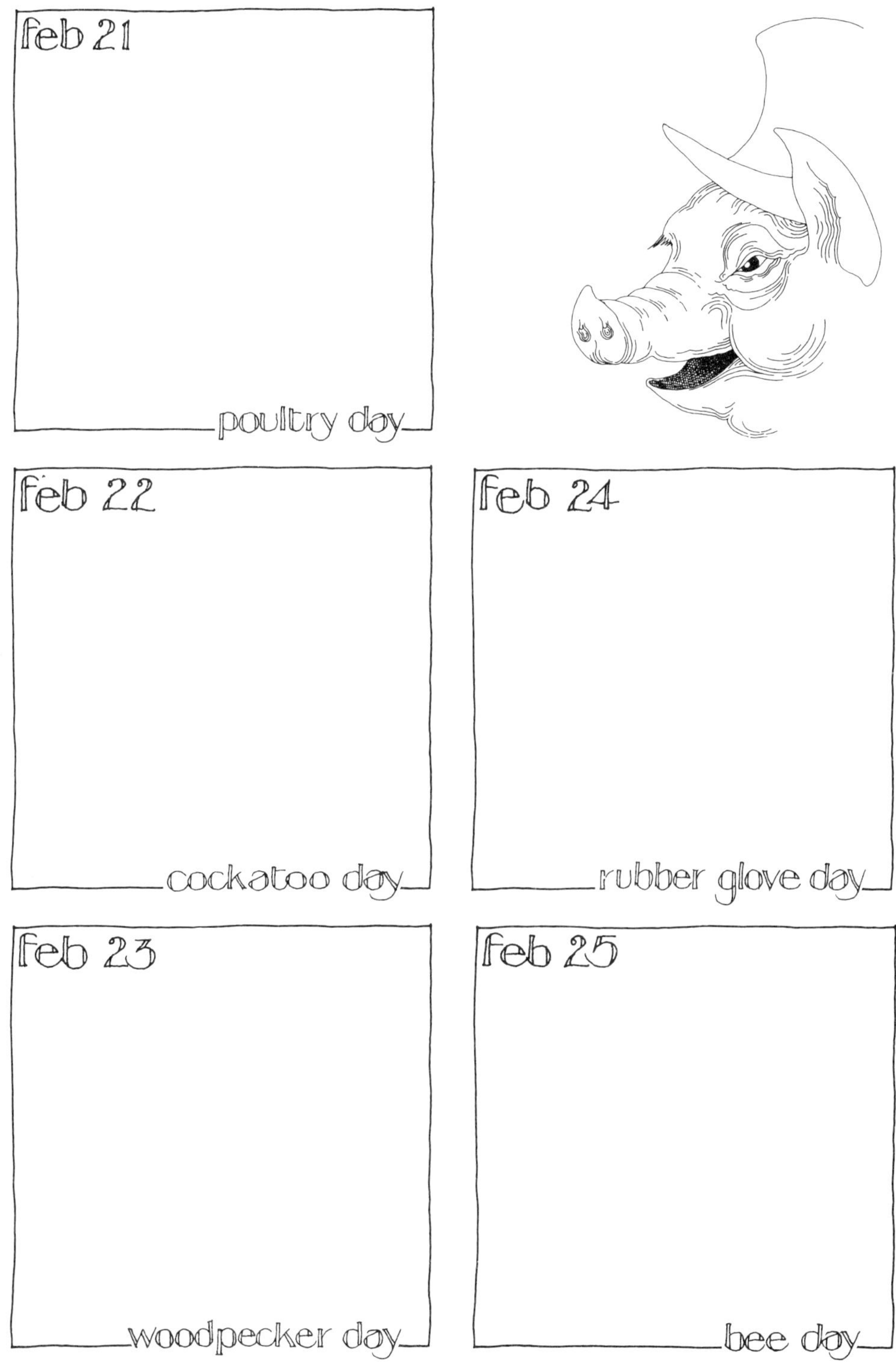

feb 21
poultry day

feb 22
cockatoo day

feb 23
woodpecker day

feb 24
rubber glove day

feb 25
bee day

feb 26

_______ space helmet day___

feb 29

_______ crab day___

feb 27

_______ mudbath day___

mar 1

_______ automobile day___

feb 28

_______ tricycle day___

mar 2

_______ toe nail day___

mar 3

teapot day

mar 4

mathematics day

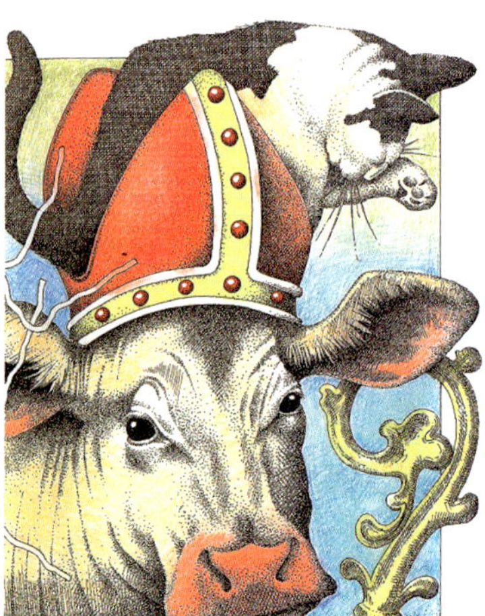

cat with sacred cow

mar 5

polar bear day

mar 6

wagging tail day

mar 7

hazelnut day

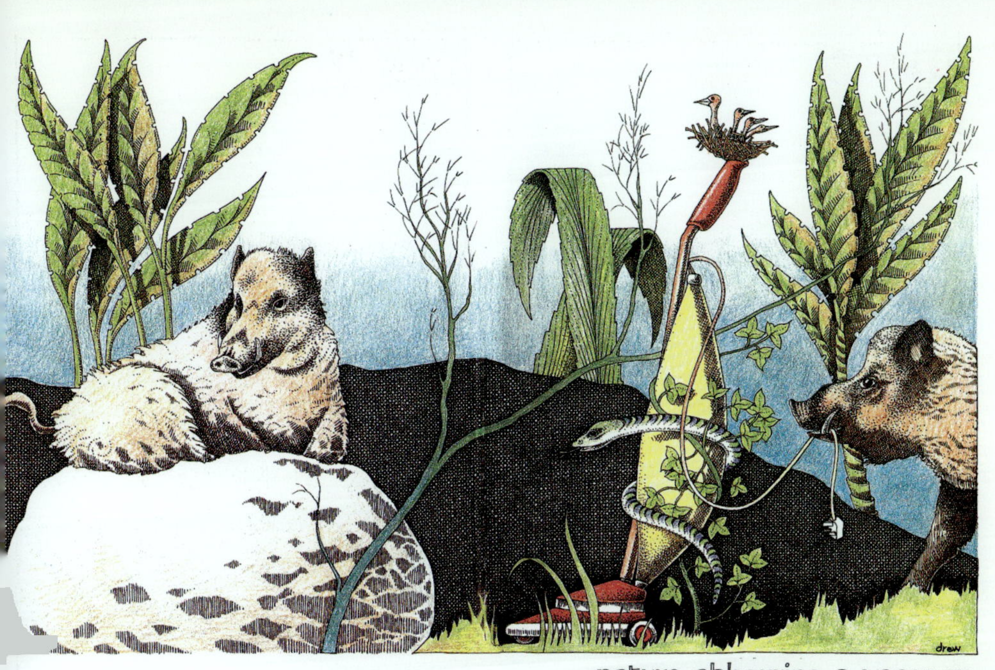

mar 8

magpie day

mar 9

maize day

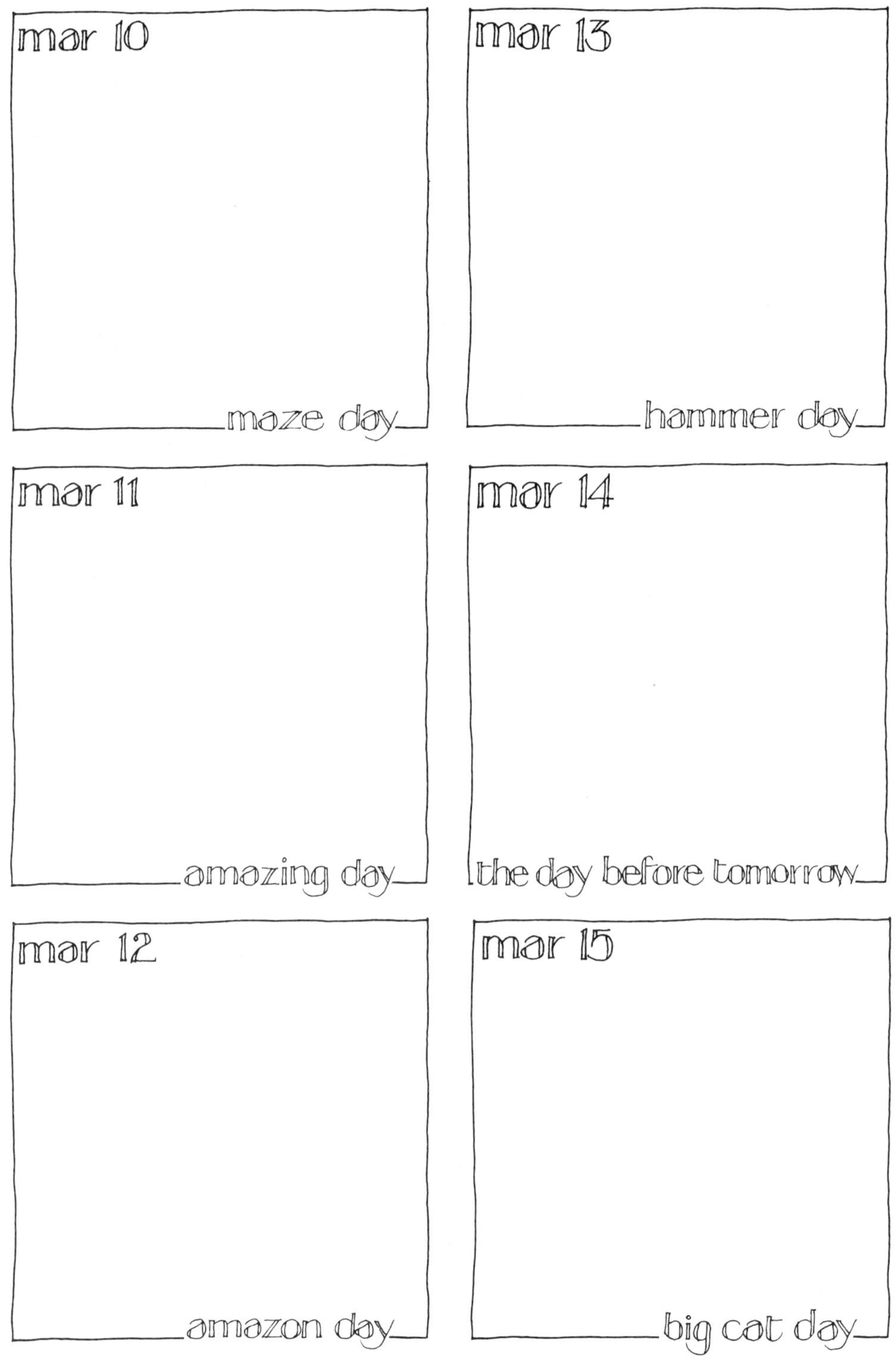

mar 10

maze day

mar 11

amazing day

mar 12

amazon day

mar 13

hammer day

mar 14

the day before tomorrow

mar 15

big cat day

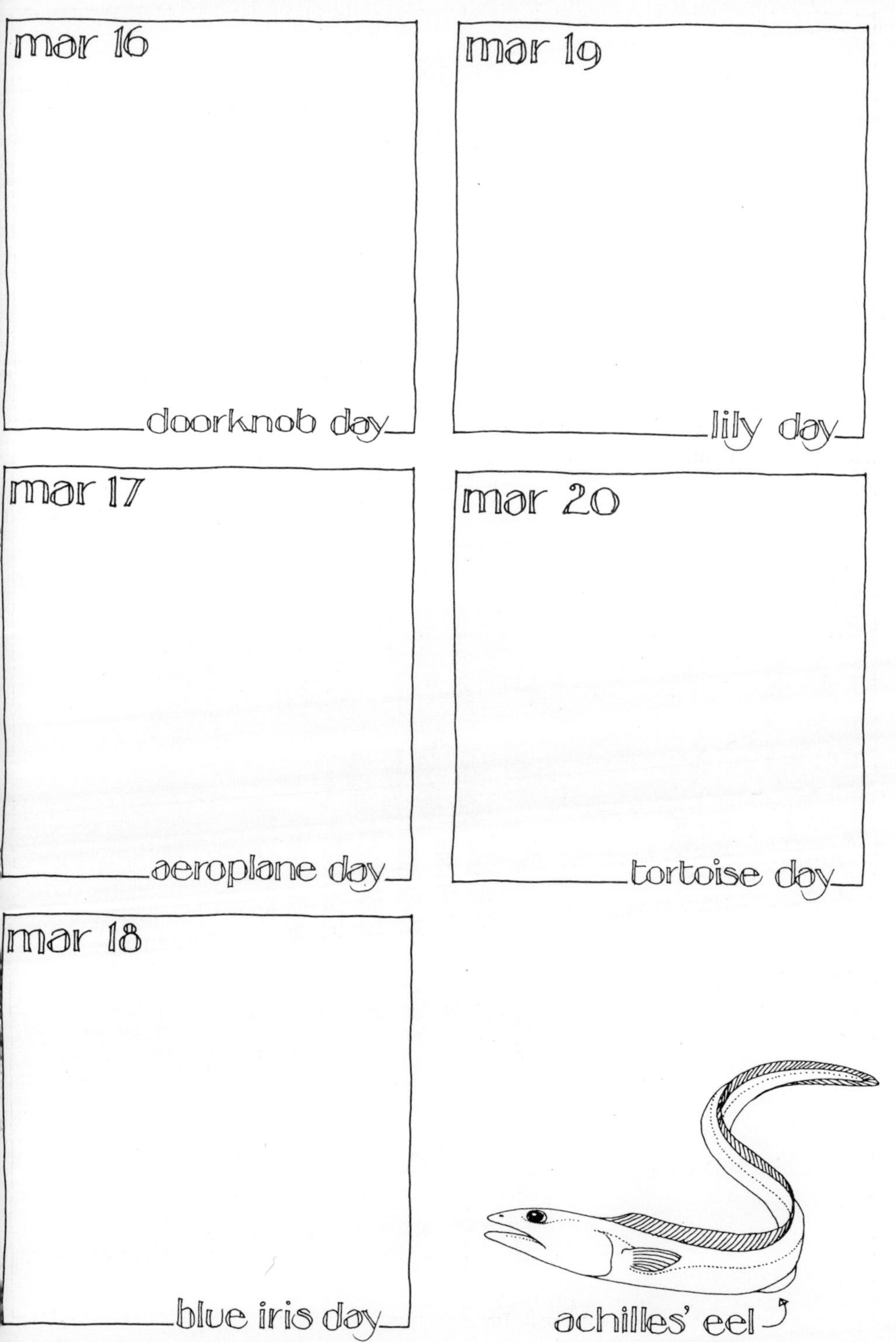

mar 16
_____doorknob day_

mar 17
_____aeroplane day_

mar 18
_____blue iris day_

mar 19
_____lily day_

mar 20
_____tortoise day_

achilles' eel

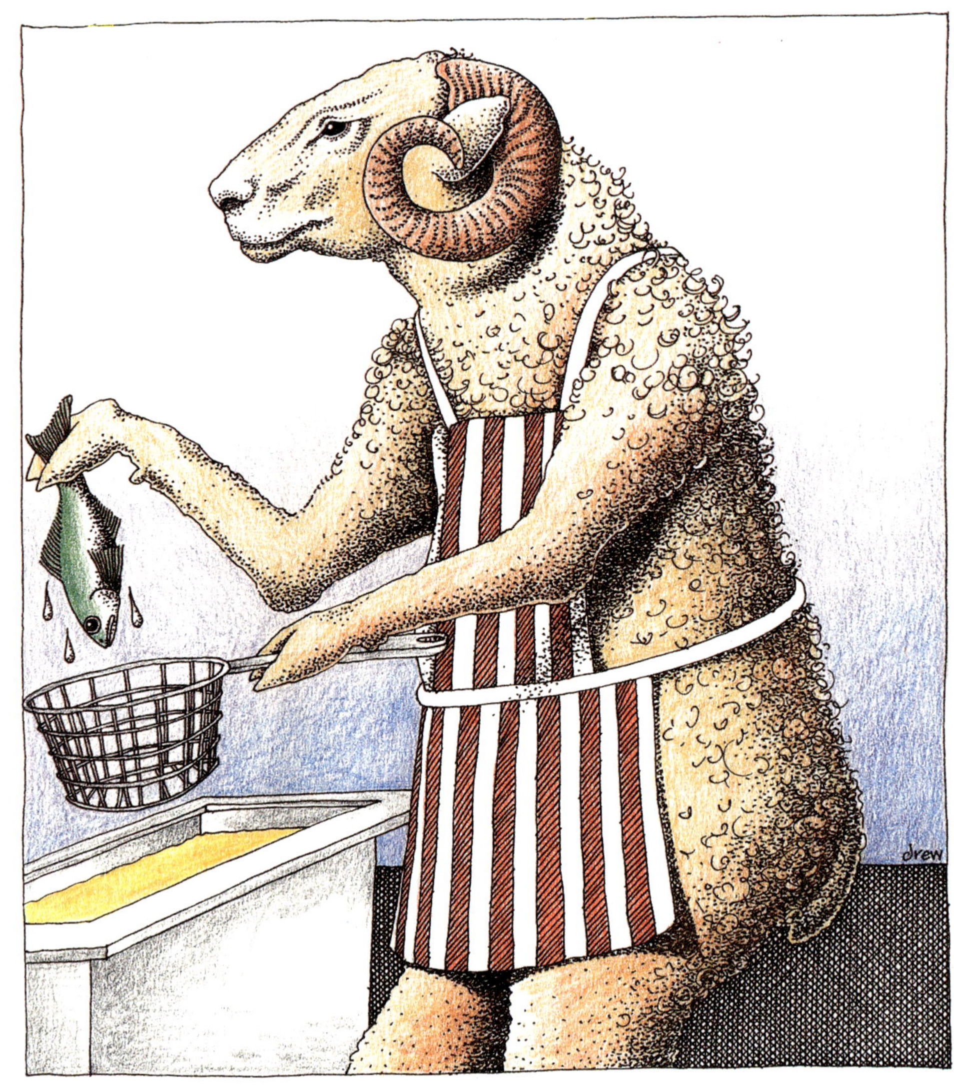

battering
ram

ARIES

Those who are born underneath this great sign
are thoughtful, successful and certain to shine.
They walk along riverbanks, head in the clouds;
they stand head and shoulders above any
                                    crowds.
They'll give their last penny to help out a friend,
here's a companion on whom to depend.
They have a bad habit that's just come to
                                    mind:
they fill in their birthdate in diaries they find.

mar 21

_______baked beans day___

mar 22

_________lollipop day___

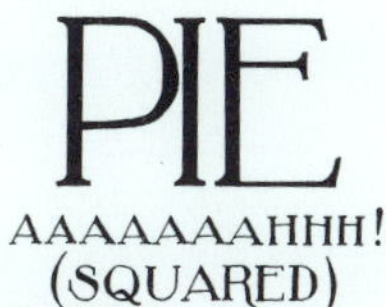

PIE
AAAAAAAHHH!
(SQUARED)

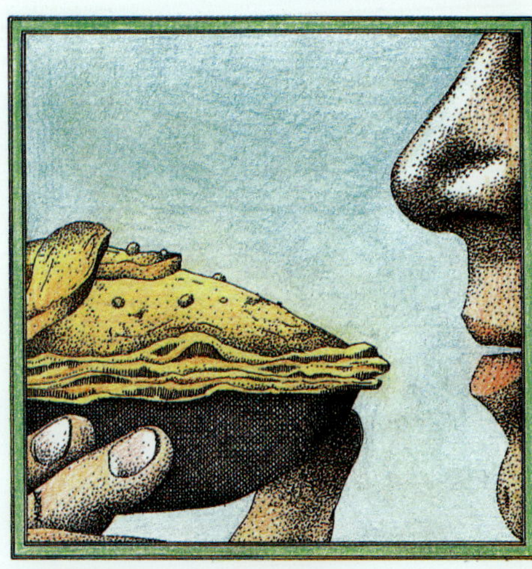

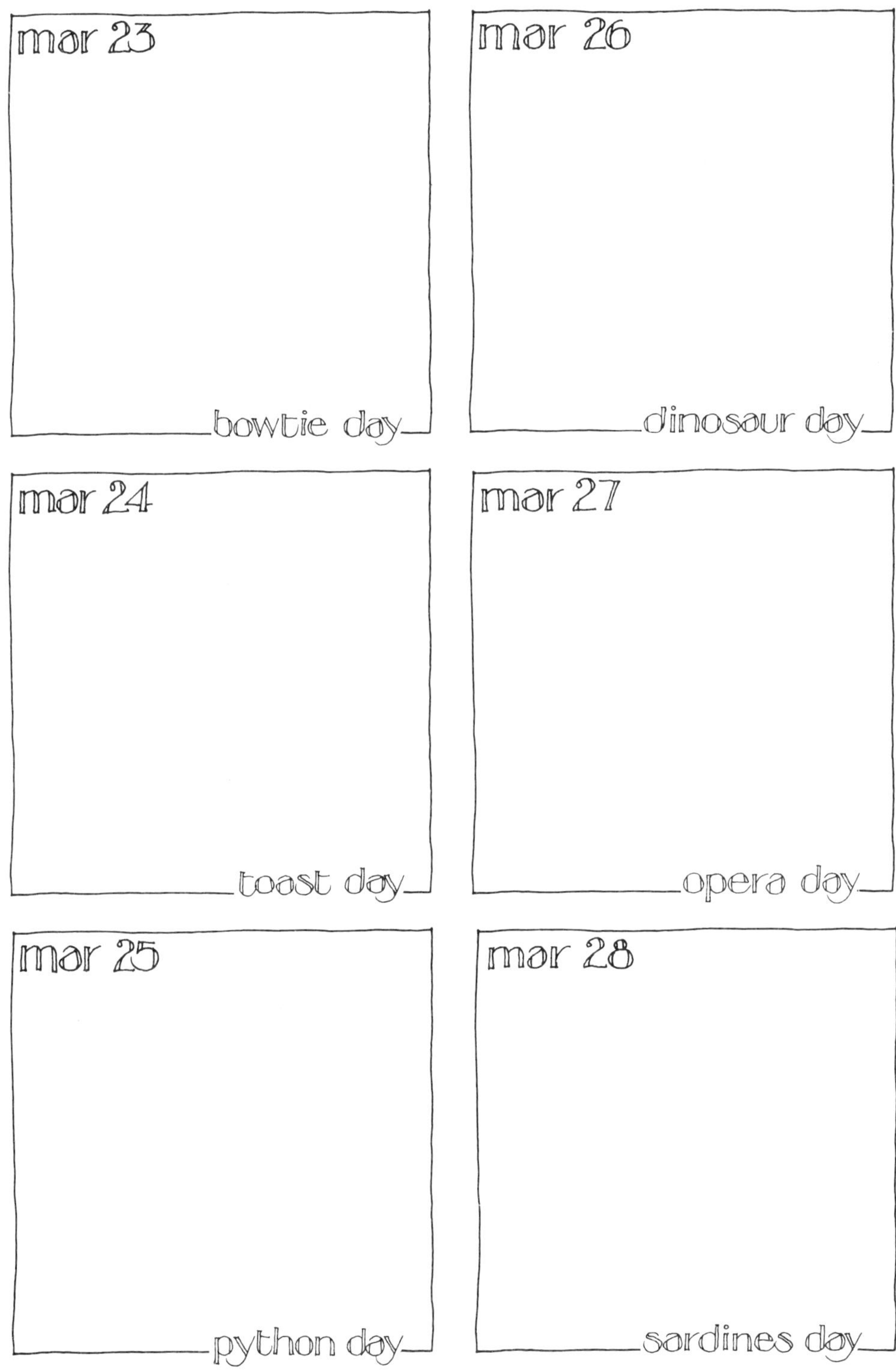

mar 23
bowtie day

mar 24
toast day

mar 25
python day

mar 26
dinosaur day

mar 27
opera day

mar 28
sardines day

mar 29

jelly day

mar 30

crossword day

mar 31

empty barrel day

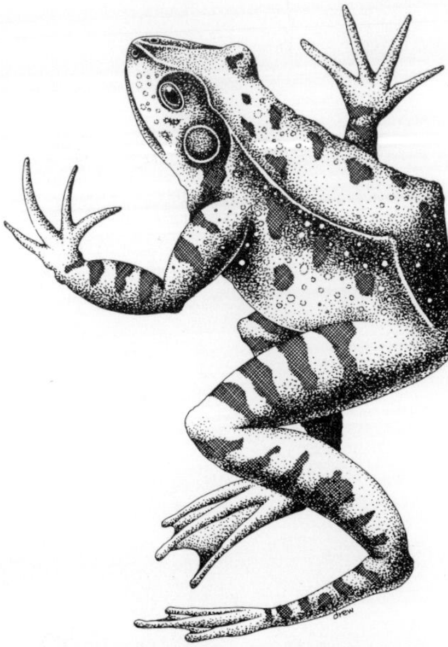

apr 1

chocolate egg day

one swallow doesn't make a summer
but a frog can make a long spring. anon

apr 2

chi hua hua day

apr 4

bulldozer day

apr 3

pistacchio day

apr 5

bullseye day

apr 6

oak day

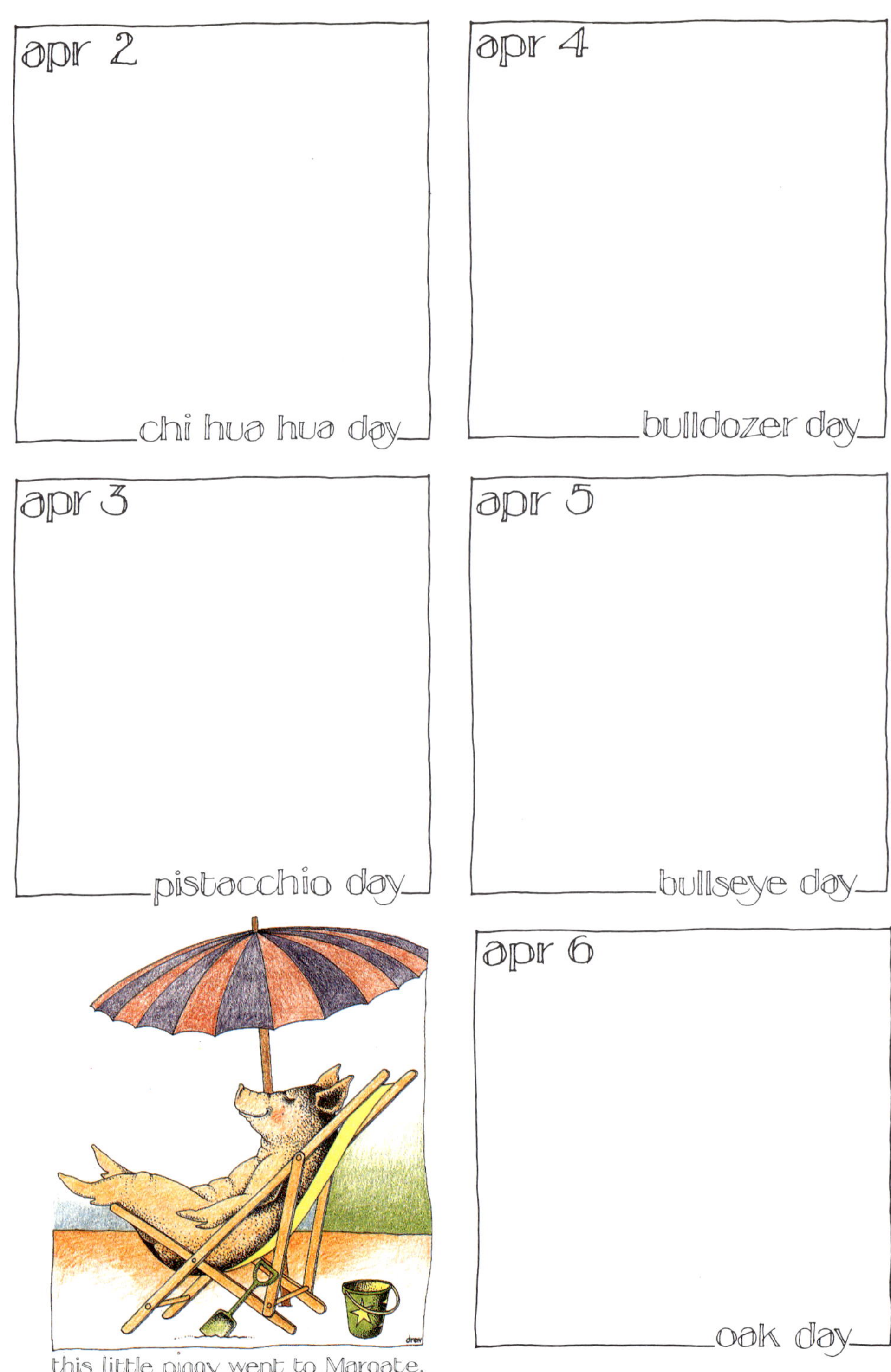

this little piggy went to Margate.

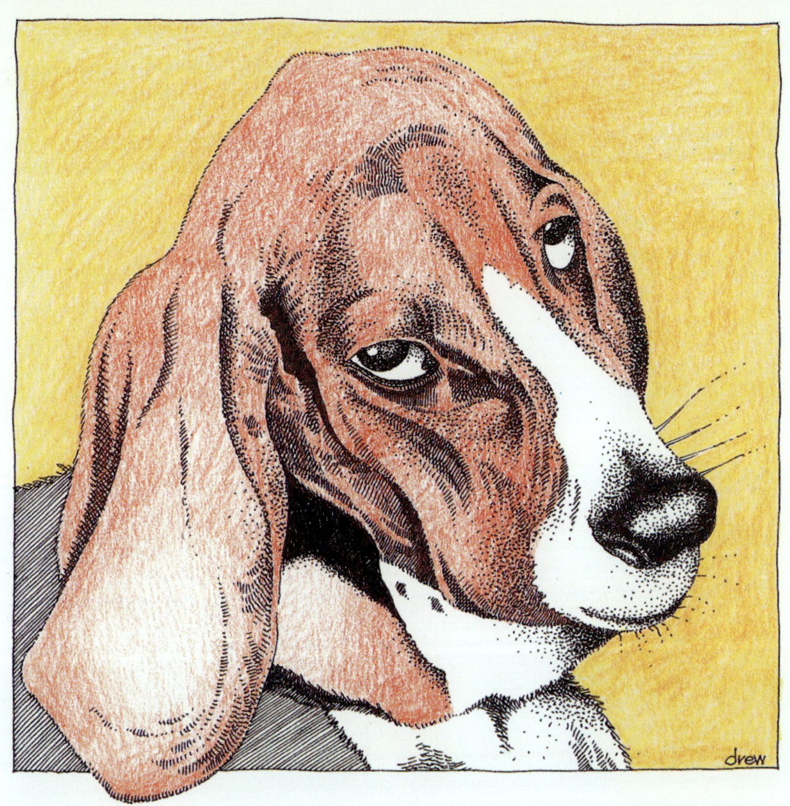

'To win back my youth, there is nothing I wouldn't do — except take exercise, get up early or be a useful member of the community.'
Oscar Wilde

apr 7

cat's paw day

apr 8

treasure day

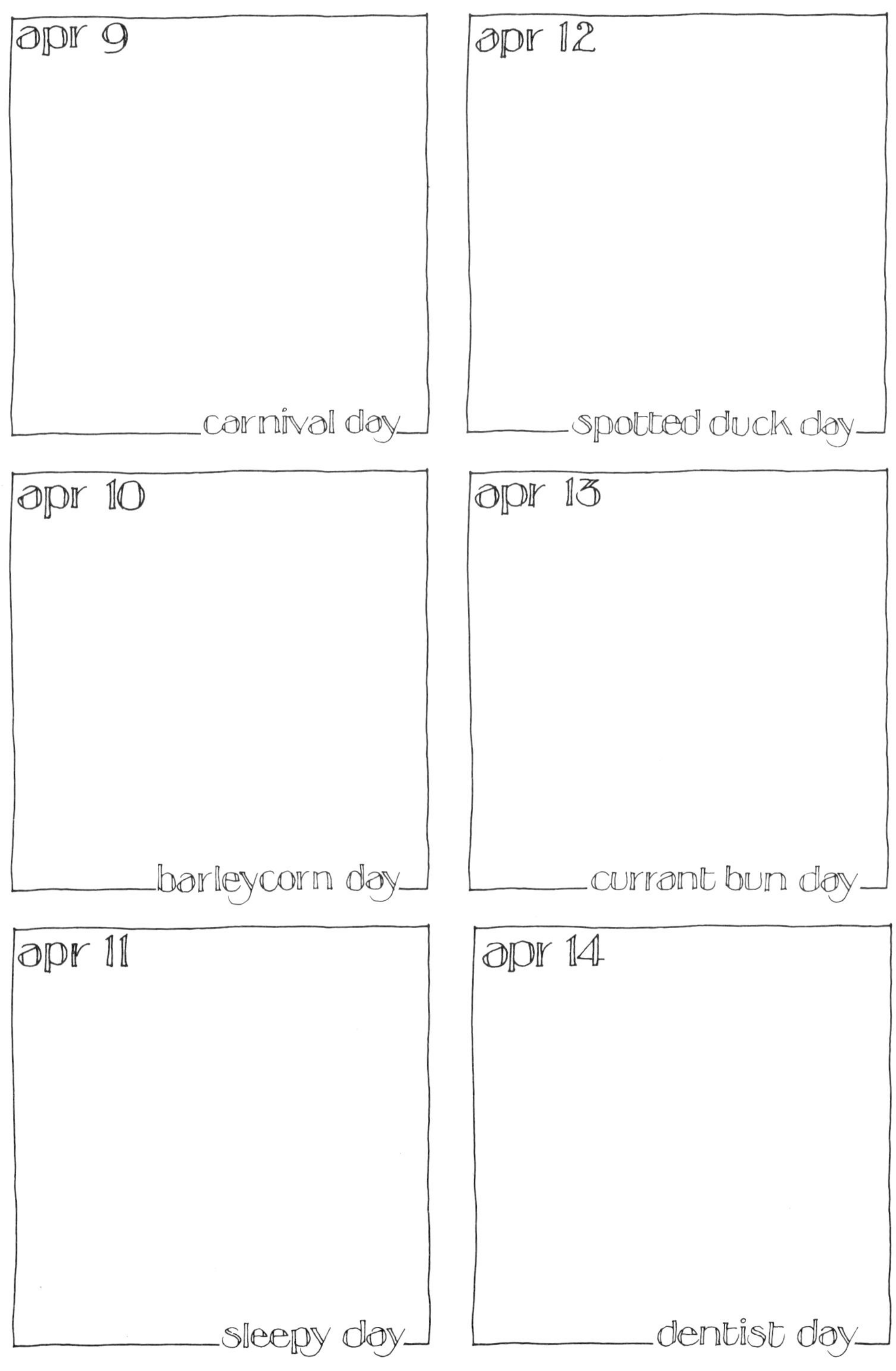

apr 9
carnival day
apr 12
spotted duck day
apr 10
barleycorn day
apr 13
currant bun day
apr 11
sleepy day
apr 14
dentist day

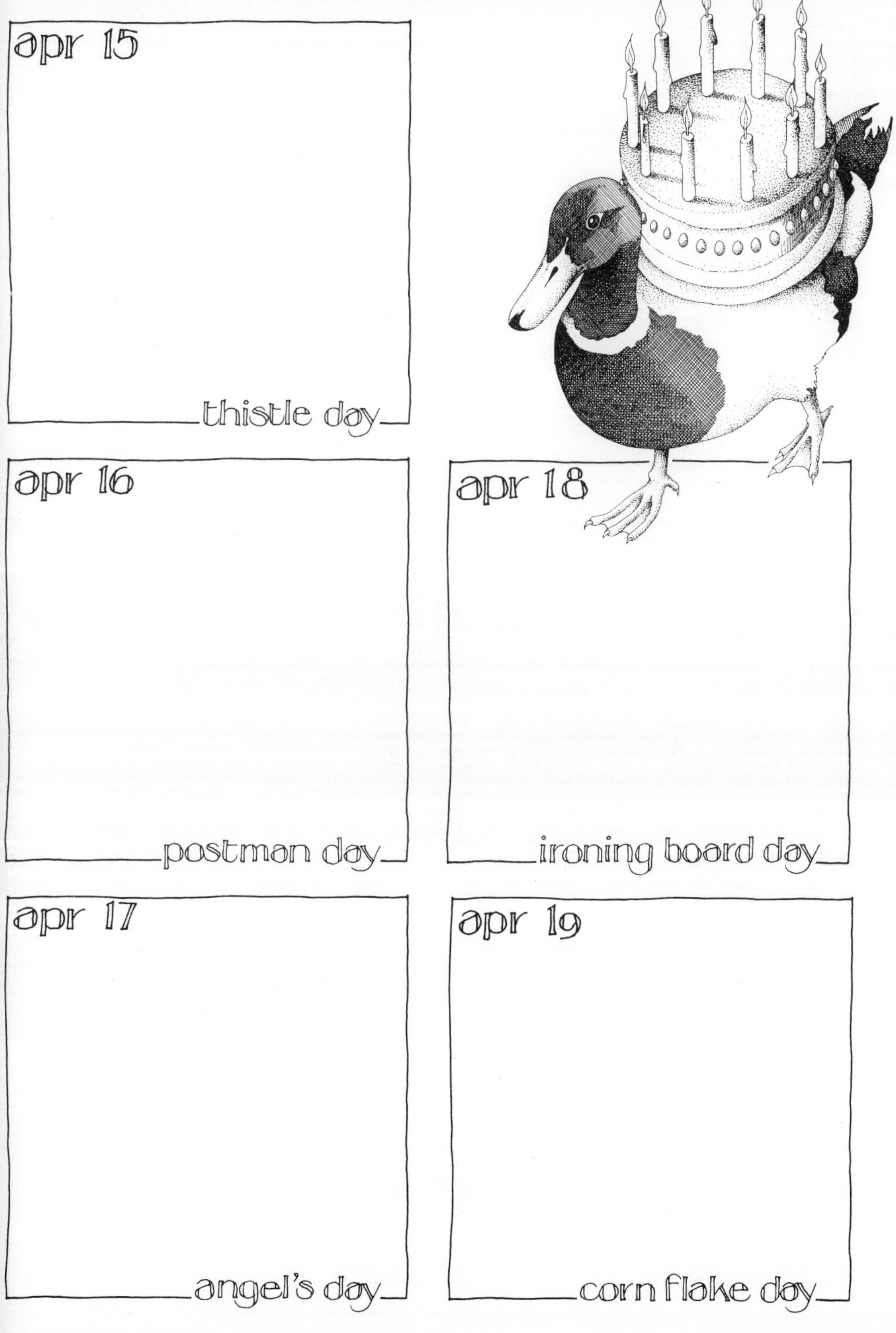

apr 15 _____ thistle day

apr 16 _____ postman day

apr 17 _____ angel's day

apr 18 _____ ironing board day

apr 19 _____ corn flake day

TAURUS
(the bull) april 20 to may 20

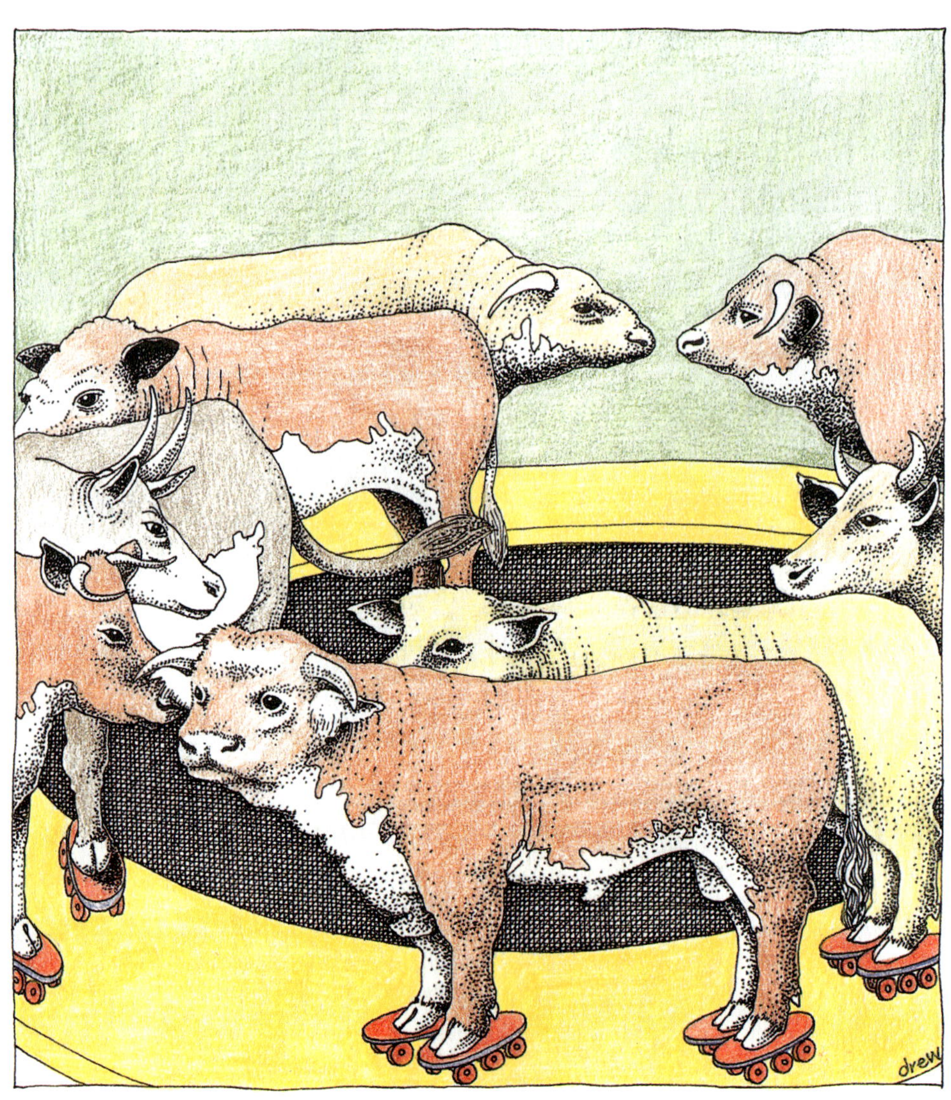

how to
keep the bull rolling

TAURUS

Those who are born underneath this great sign
are thoughtful, successful and certain to shine.
Their gardens are fruitful, their houses are neat;
tell them a secret, you'll find they're discreet,
But show them a spider, they'll run for a mile:
how can arachnids become such a trial?
Fashion's an interest they haven't explored:
they've tried to be stylish but only get bored.

apr 20

_______ mouse day _______

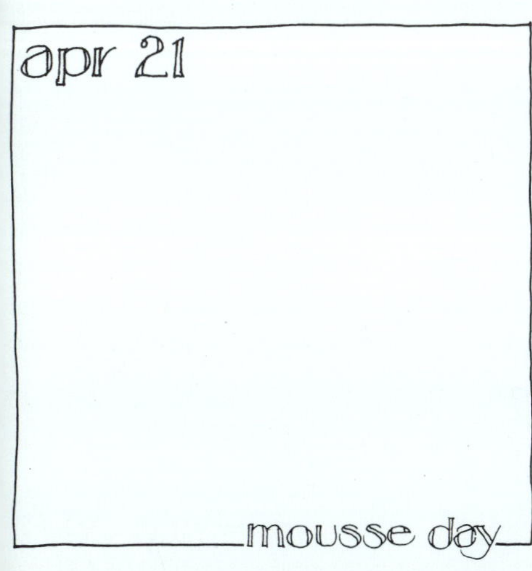

apr 21

_______ mousse day _______

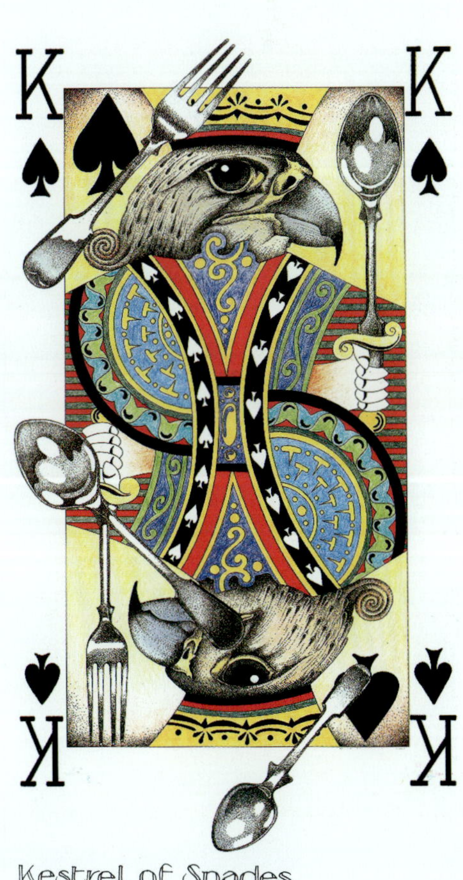

Kestrel of Spades

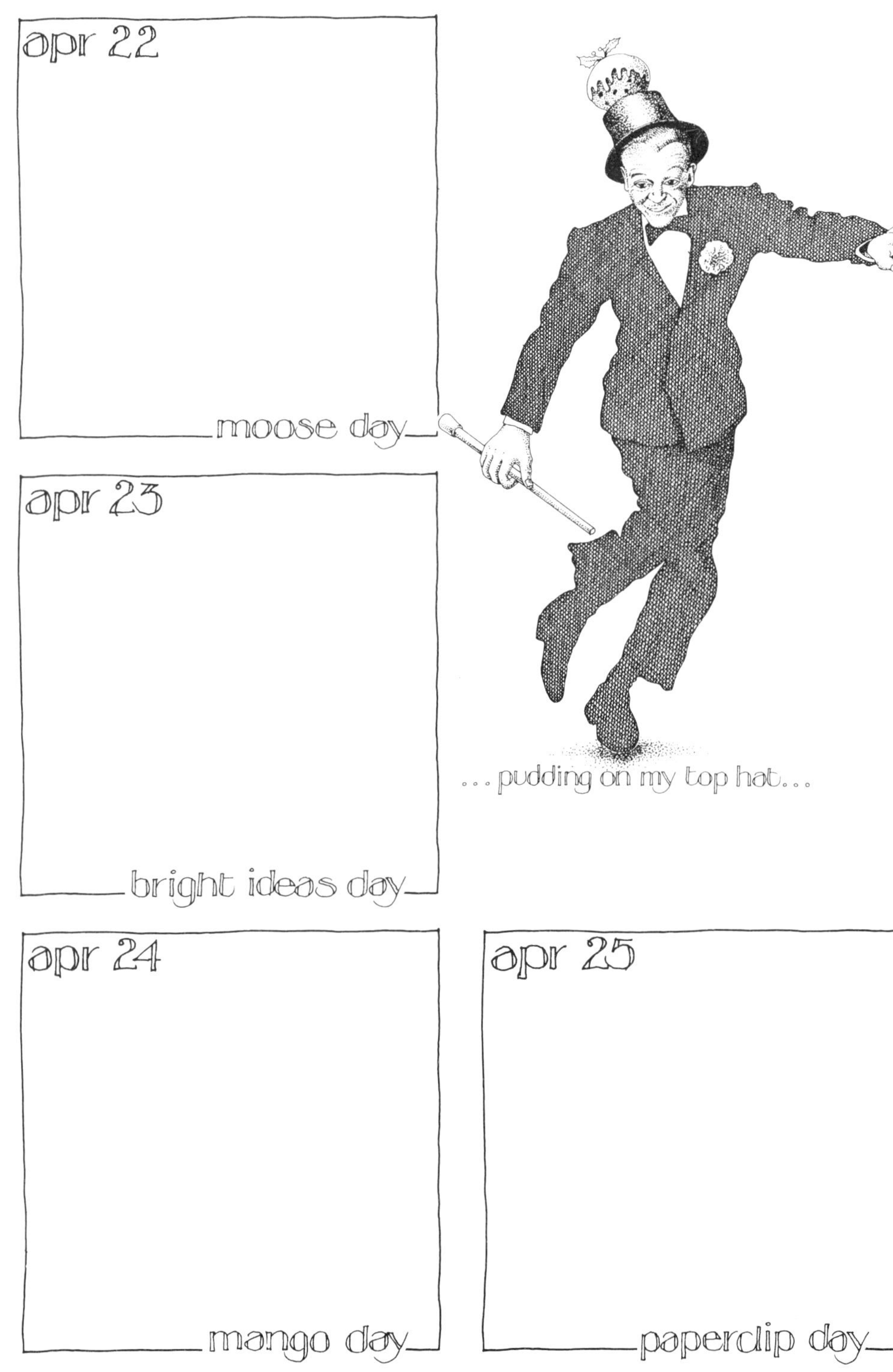

apr 22

___ moose day___

apr 23

___ bright ideas day___

apr 24

___ mango day___

apr 25

___ paperclip day___

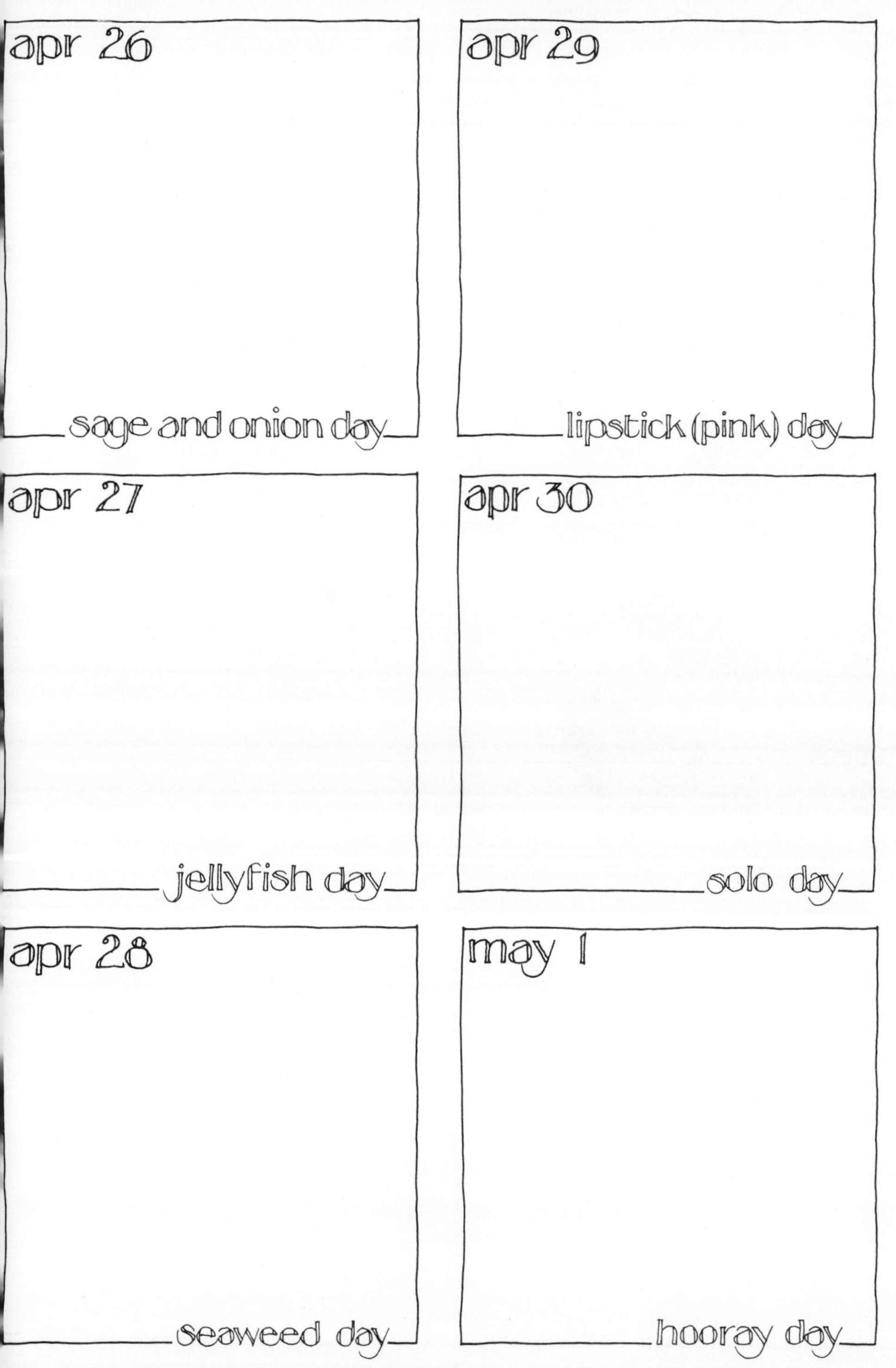
apr 26
sage and onion day

apr 29
lipstick (pink) day

apr 27
jellyfish day

apr 30
solo day

apr 28
seaweed day

may 1
hooray day

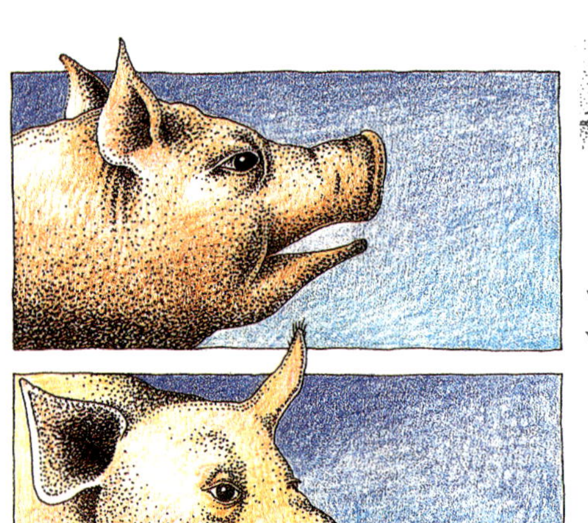

what do we
want ?

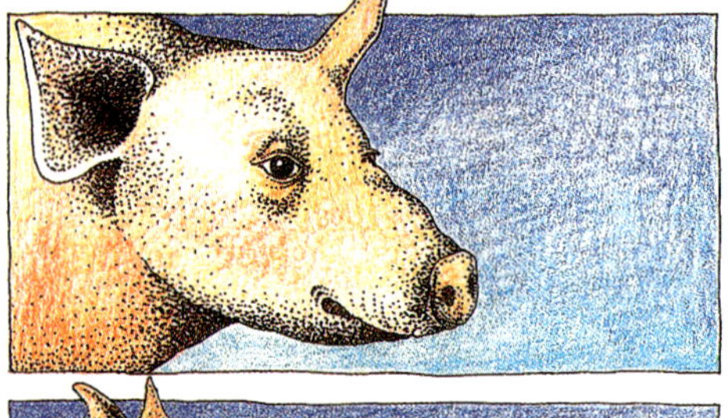

procrastination

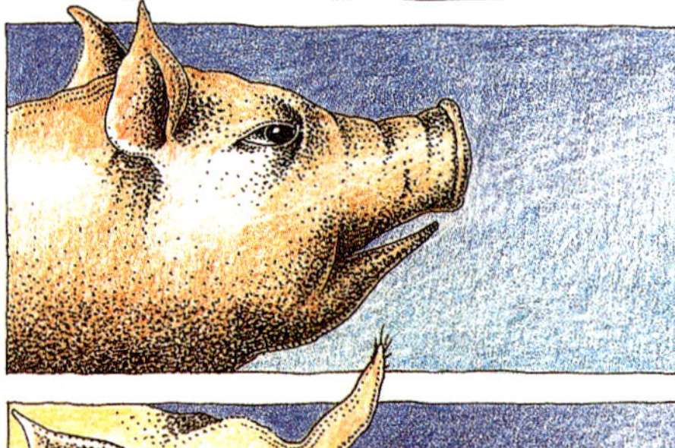

when do we
want it ?

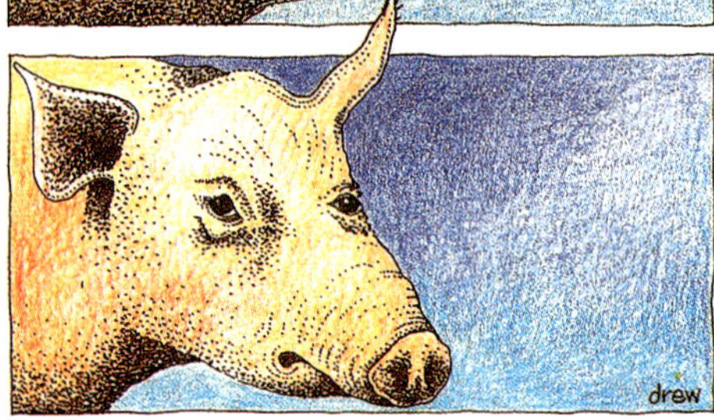

next week

may 2

_____ tall ship day_

may 3

_____________ kite day_

may 4

brussels.sprout day

may 5

nutmeg day

may 6

orangeade day

may 7

blue danube day

may 8

gooseberry day

may 9

golden delicious day

may 10

bronze day

may 11

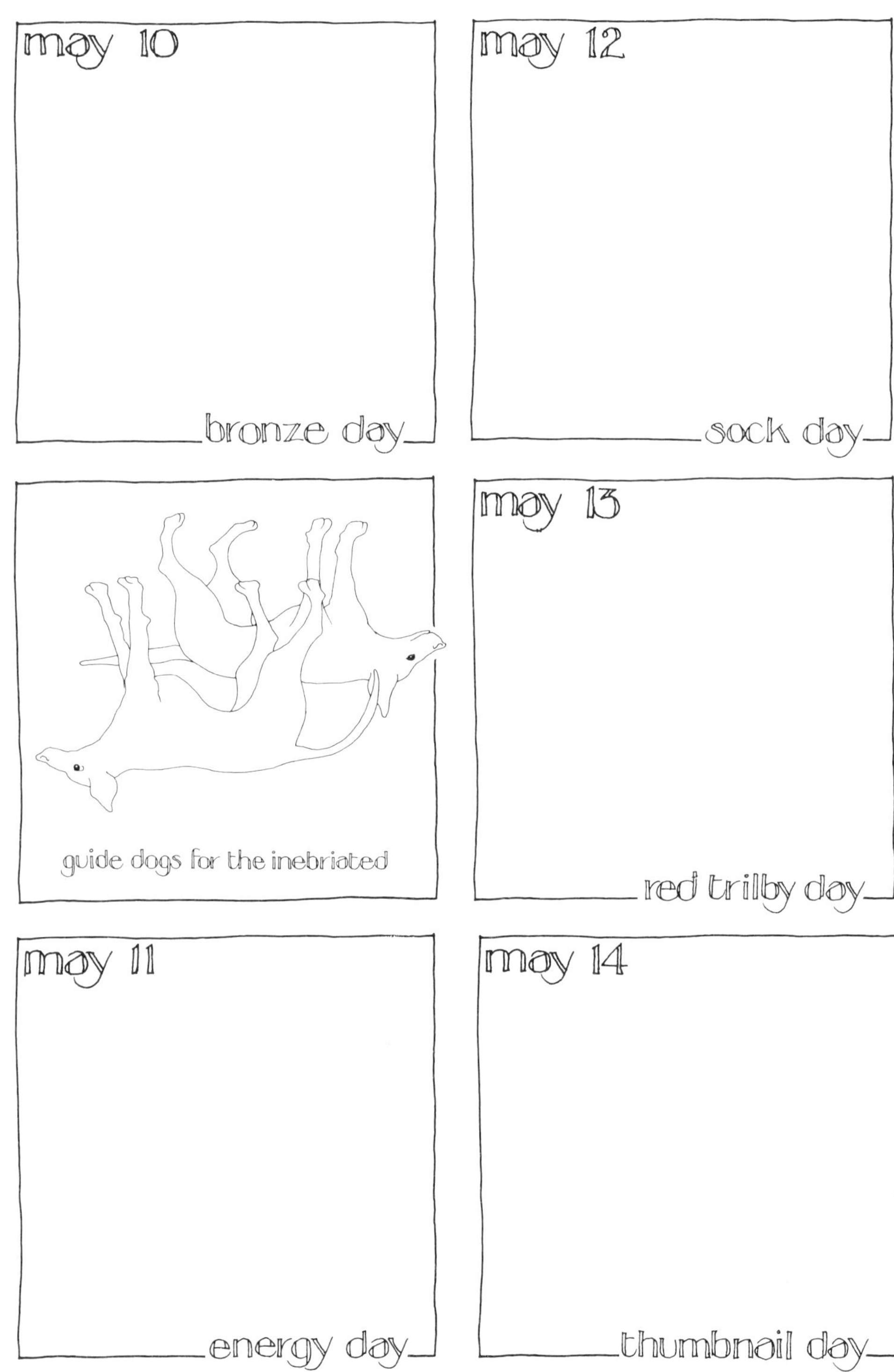

energy day

may 12

sock day

may 13

red trilby day

may 14

thumbnail day

may 15

mirror day

may 16

gorgonzola day

may 17

pigsty day

may 18

football day

may 19

tomato soup day

may 20

sauna day

GEMINI
(the twins) may 21 to june 21

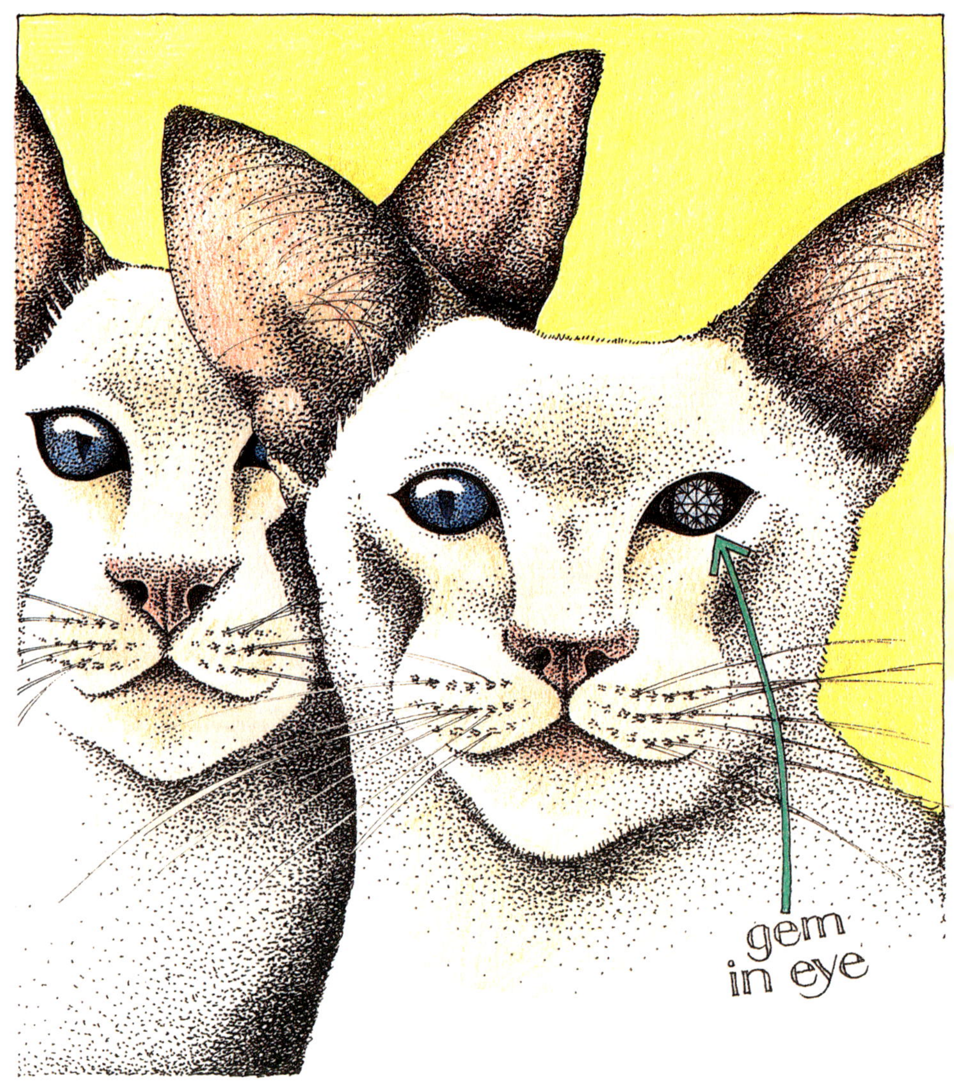

siamese
twin

GEMINI

Those who are born underneath this great sign
are thoughtful, successful and certain to shine.
They love mathematics and hate rosé wine;
give them a doughnut, they think it's divine.
Their greatest desire is a snooze by the fire
while spitting out cherry pips, higher and
higher.

Give them a Sunday, they'll shampoo the car;
give them a Friday, they'll prop up the bar.

may 21

foxglove day

may 22

waterfall day

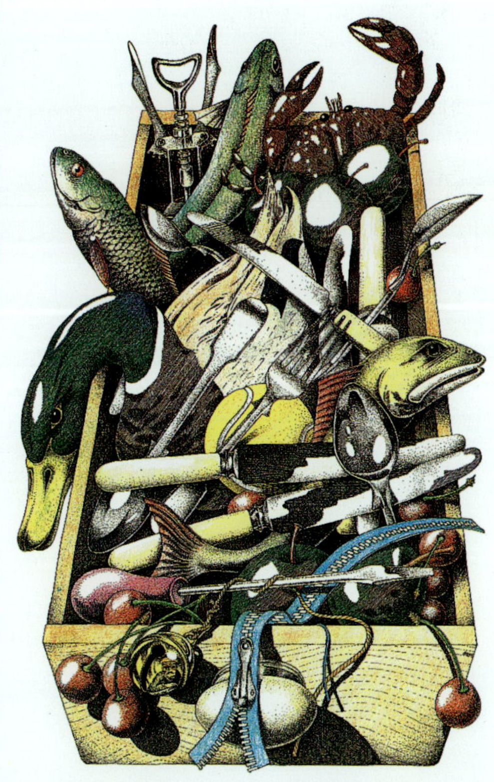

Lenny's Drawer

may 23
desert day

may 24
dessert day

may 25
tractor day

may 26
white tulip day

may 27
white hart day

may 28
white lace day

may 29	jun 1
_______ cooks day_	_______ red carpet day_
may 30	jun 2
_______ daisy day_	_______ pie day_
may 31	jun 3
_______ nurse day_	_______ bramble jelly day_

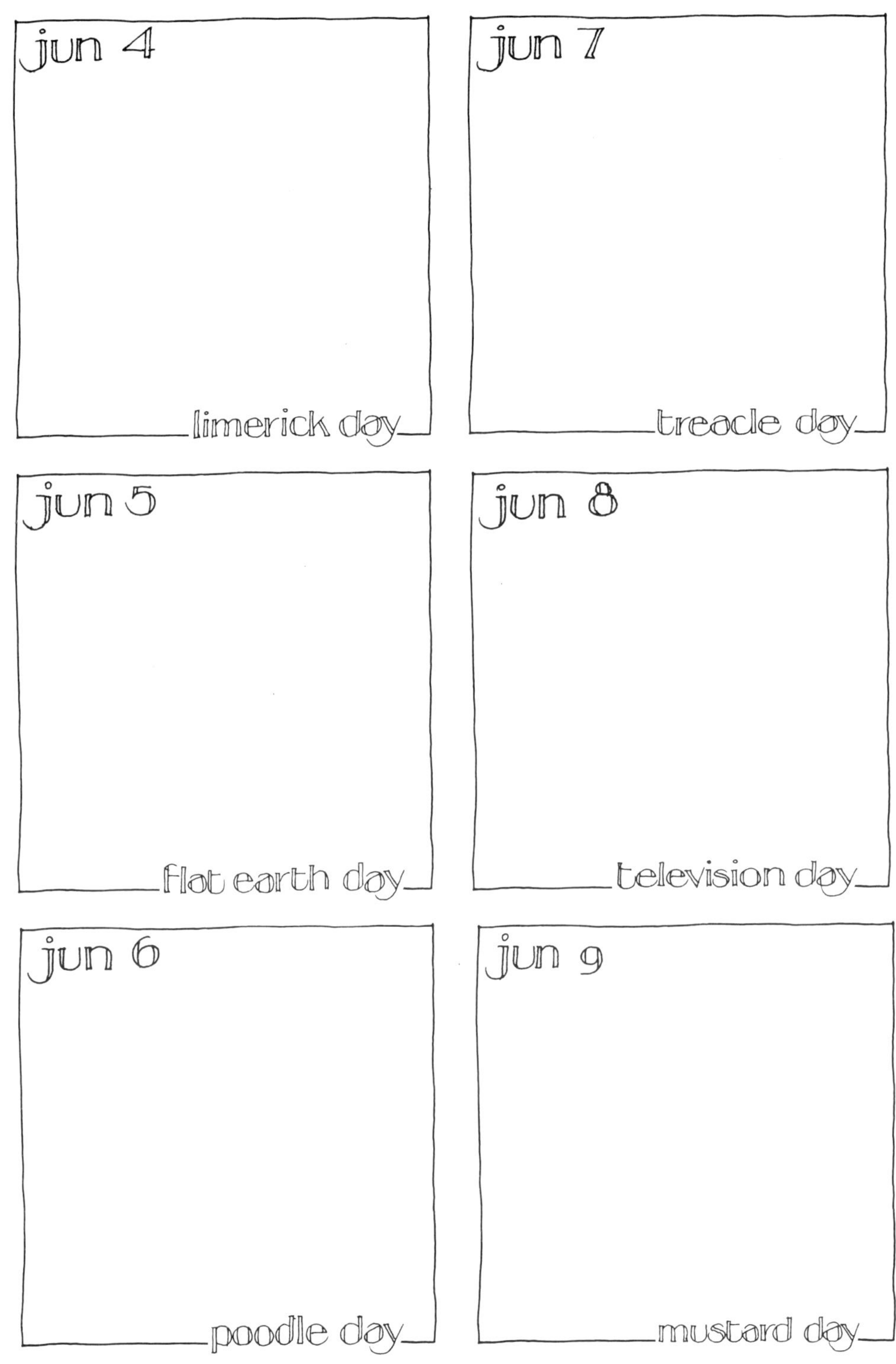

jun 4
limerick day

jun 5
flat earth day

jun 6
poodle day

jun 7
treacle day

jun 8
television day

jun 9
mustard day

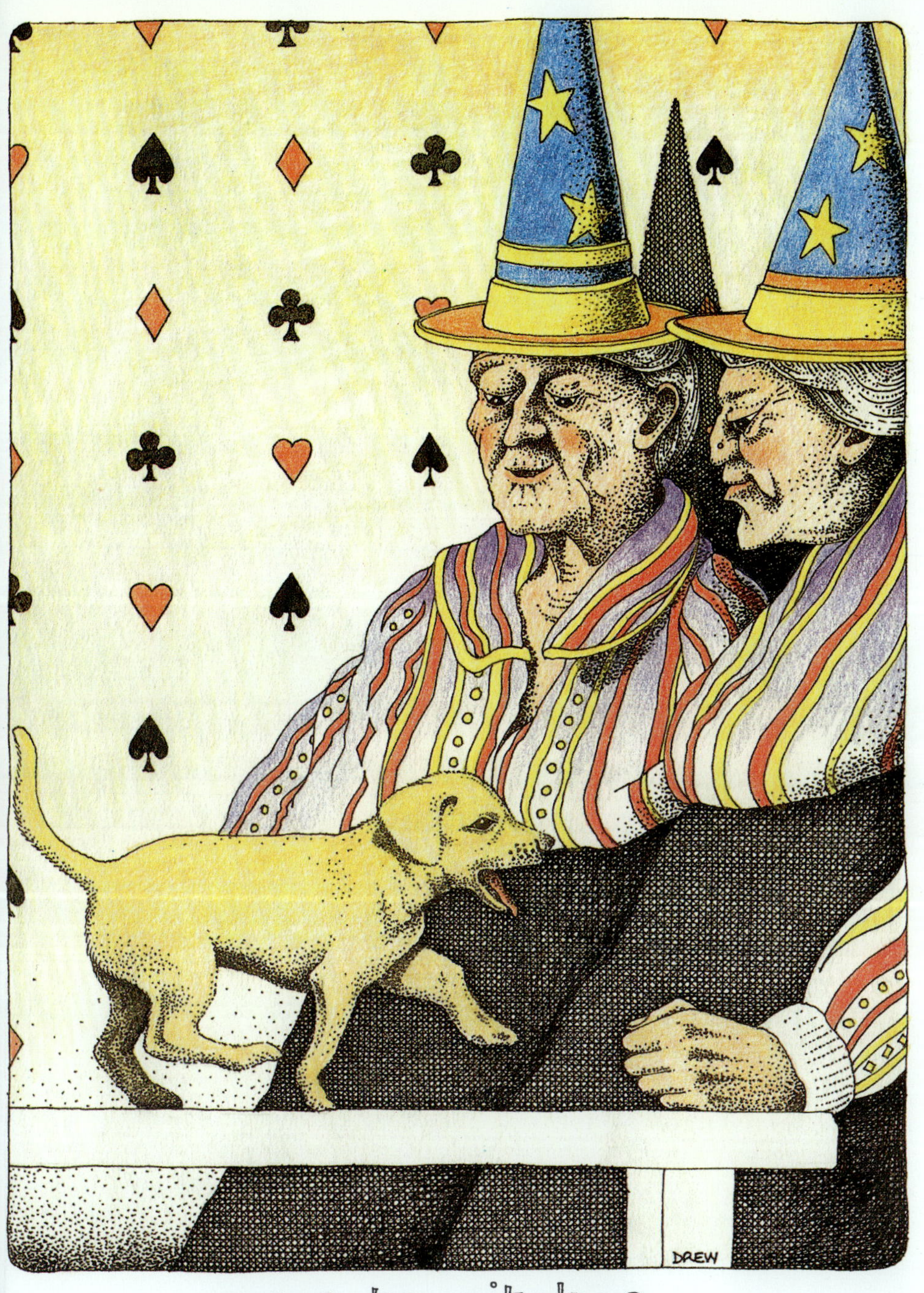

wags to witches

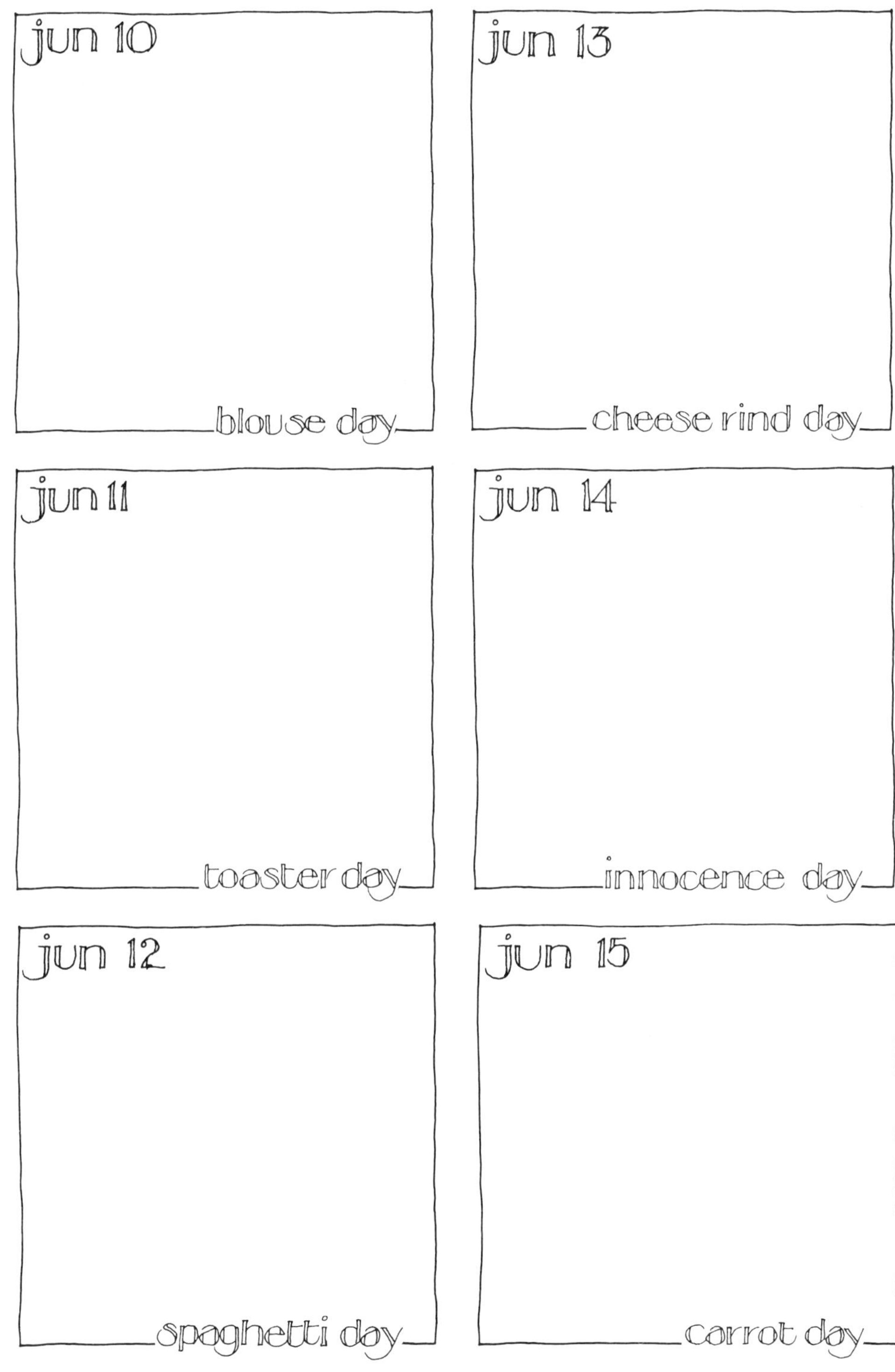

jun 10
blouse day

jun 13
cheese rind day

jun 11
toaster day

jun 14
innocence day

jun 12
spaghetti day

jun 15
carrot day

jun 16

__________ shovel (red) day__

jun 19

__________ gerbil day__

jun 17

__________ fish pie day__

jun 20

__________ infra red day__

jun 18

__________ apple pip day__

jun 21

__________ labrador day__

CANCER
(the crab) june 22 to july 22

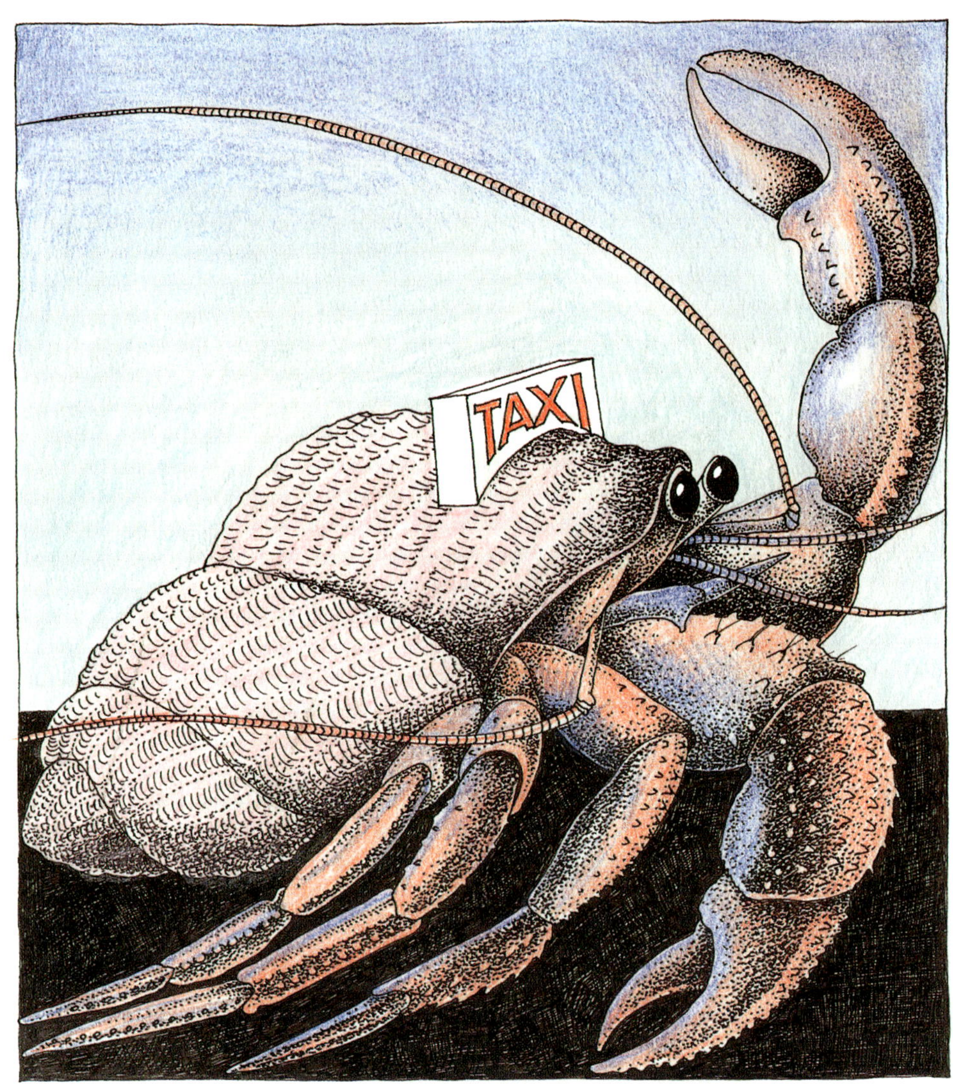

taxi crab

CANCER

Those who are born underneath this great sign
are thoughtful, successful and certain to shine.
They never wear raincoats, despite heavy rain:
(they're soaked to the skin, but they'll do it
                                again).
Their politics vary according to friends;
they think there's a god, for it ties up
                                loose ends.
They never wear trousers, unless it's in Lent;
they'll eat a banana, unless it is bent.

jun 22

firework day

jun 24

rice pudding day

jun 23

gangplank day

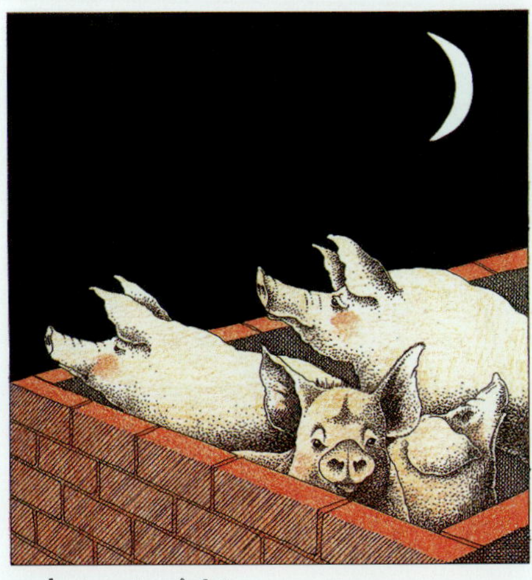

red sty at night

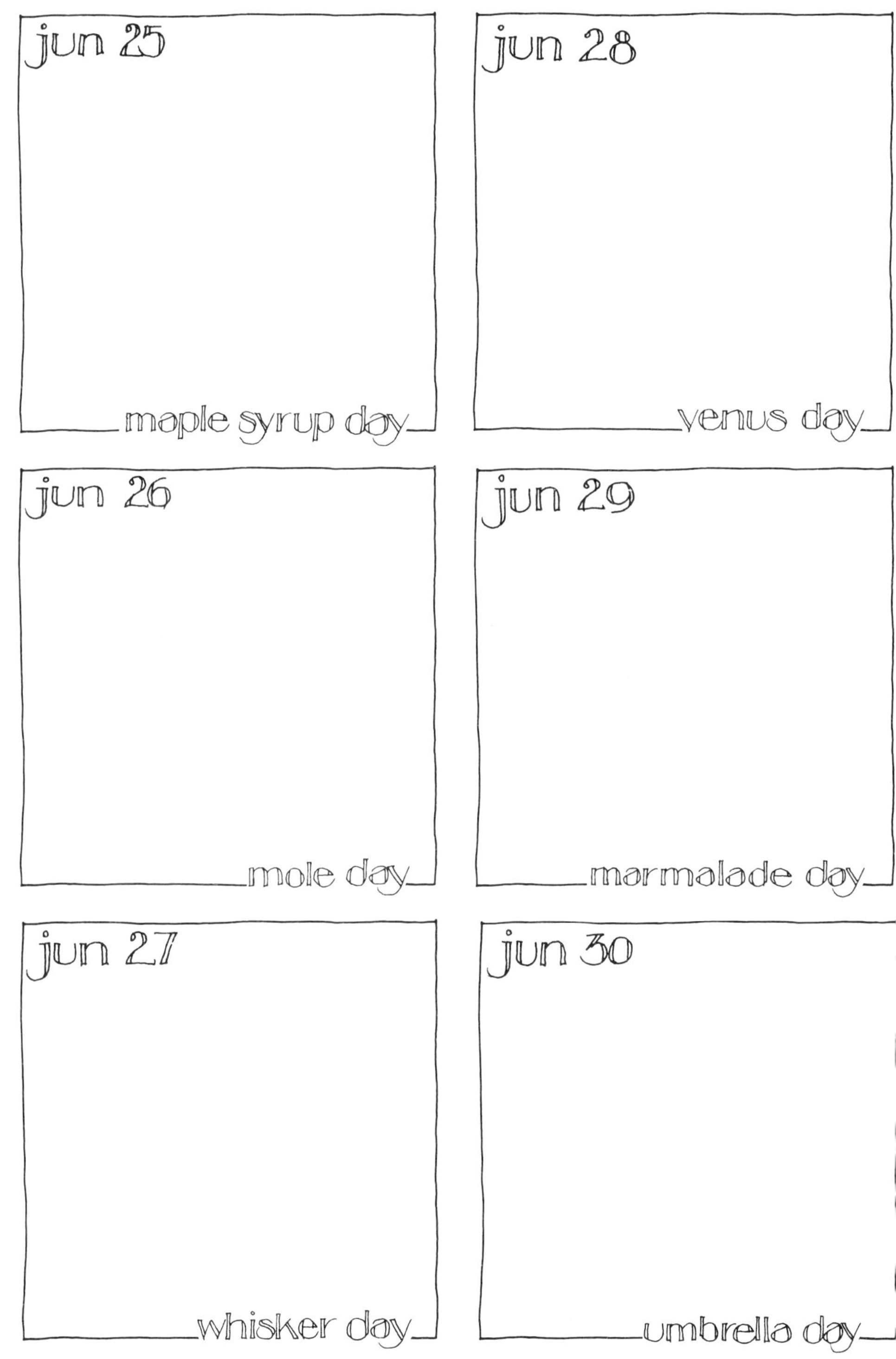

jun 25
maple syrup day

jun 28
venus day

jun 26
mole day

jun 29
marmalade day

jun 27
whisker day

jun 30
umbrella day

jul 1

_______ high heels_

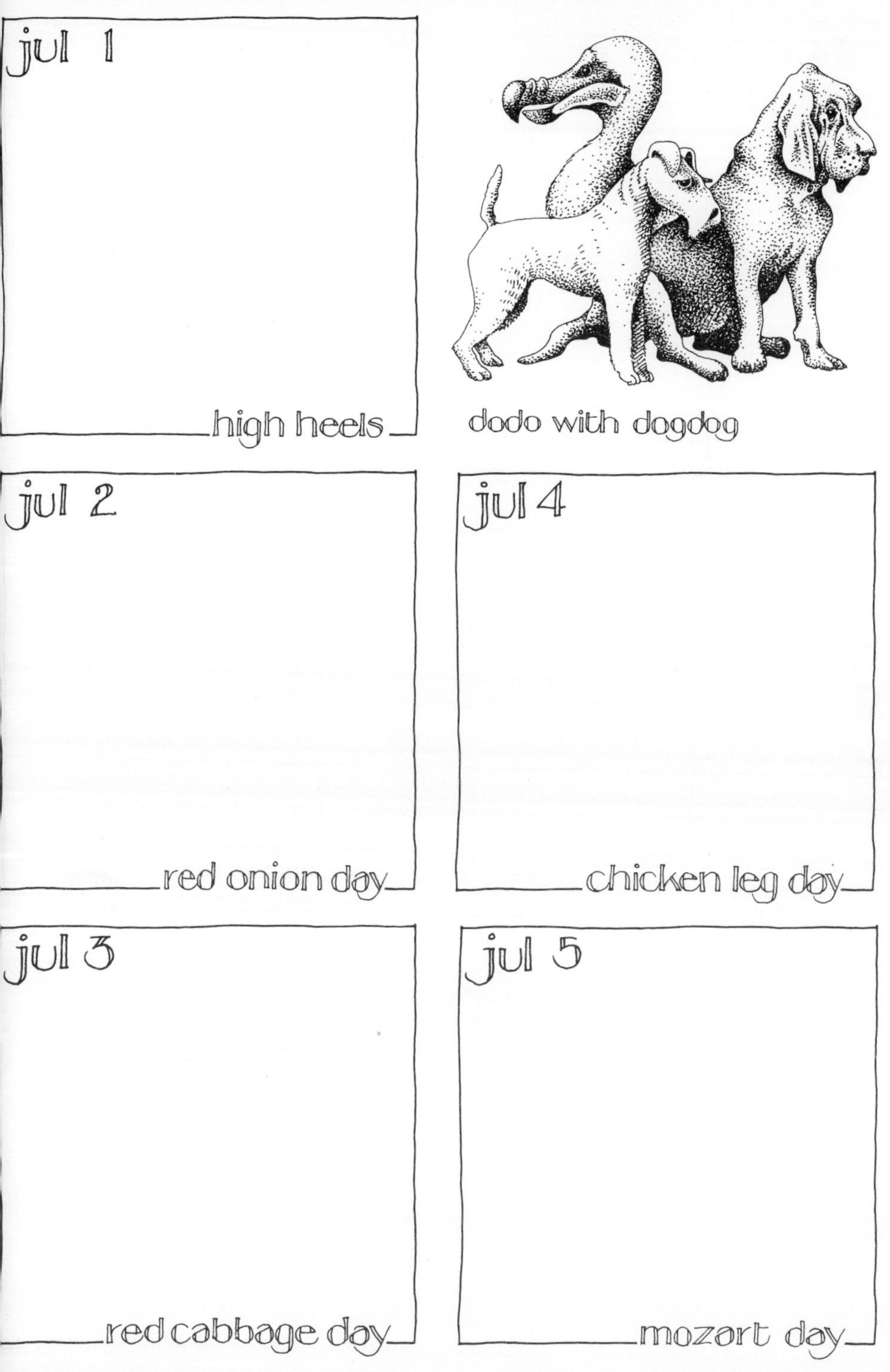

dodo with dogdog

jul 2

_______ red onion day_

jul 3

_______ red cabbage day_

jul 4

_______ chicken leg day_

jul 5

_______ mozart day_

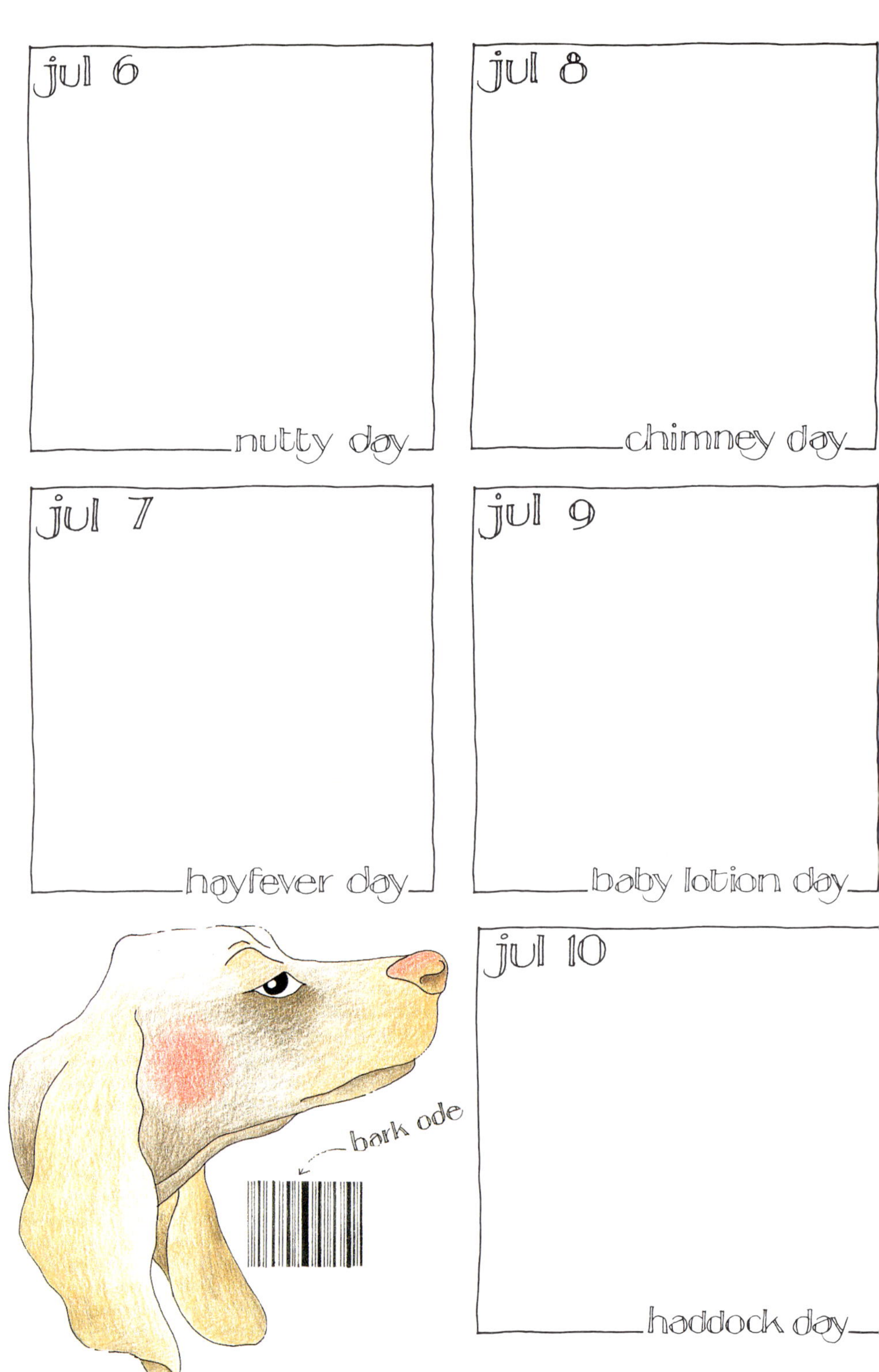

jul 6
nutty day
jul 8
chimney day
jul 7
hayfever day
jul 9
baby lotion day
jul 10
haddock day
bark ode

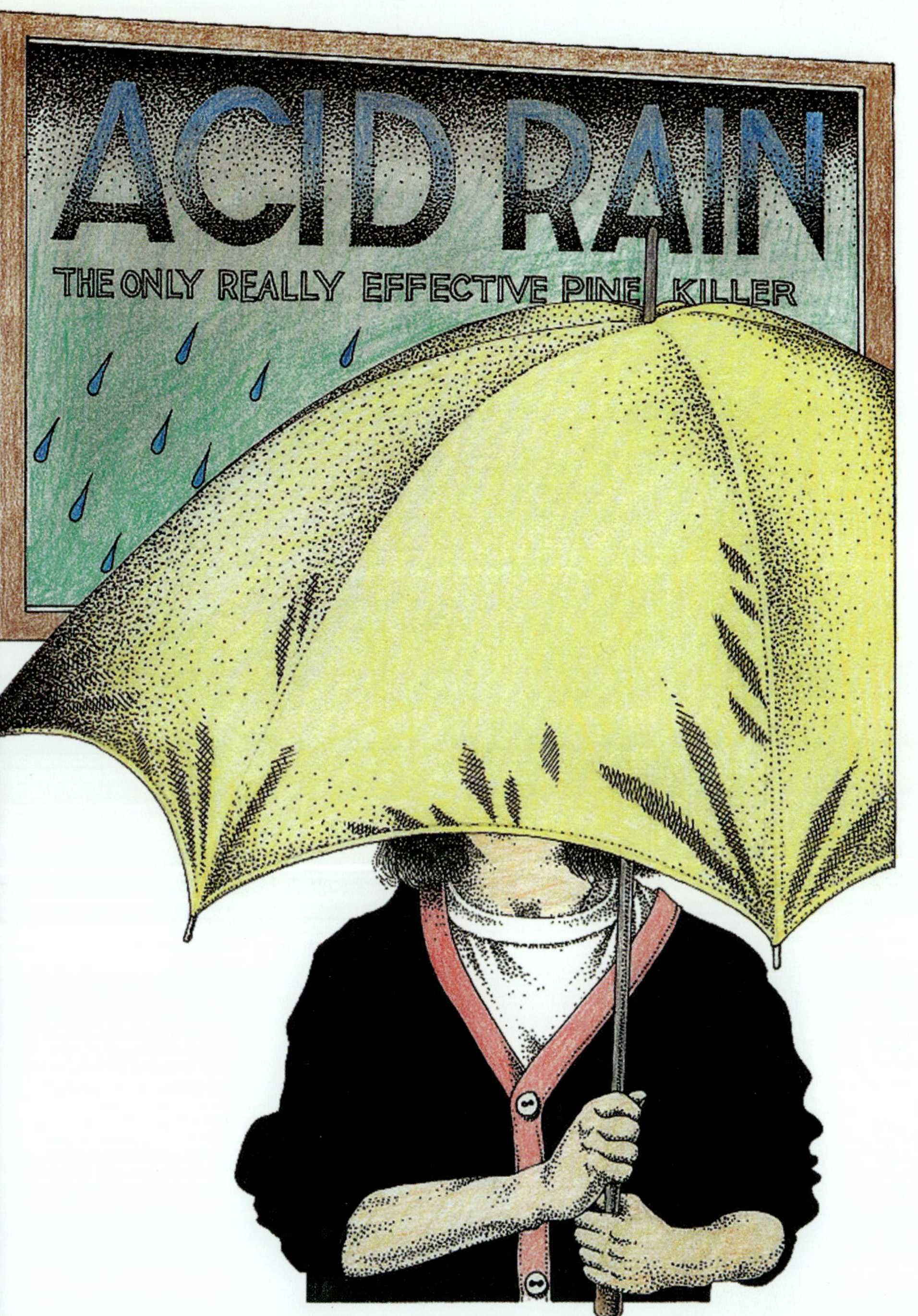

ACID RAIN
THE ONLY REALLY EFFECTIVE PINE KILLER

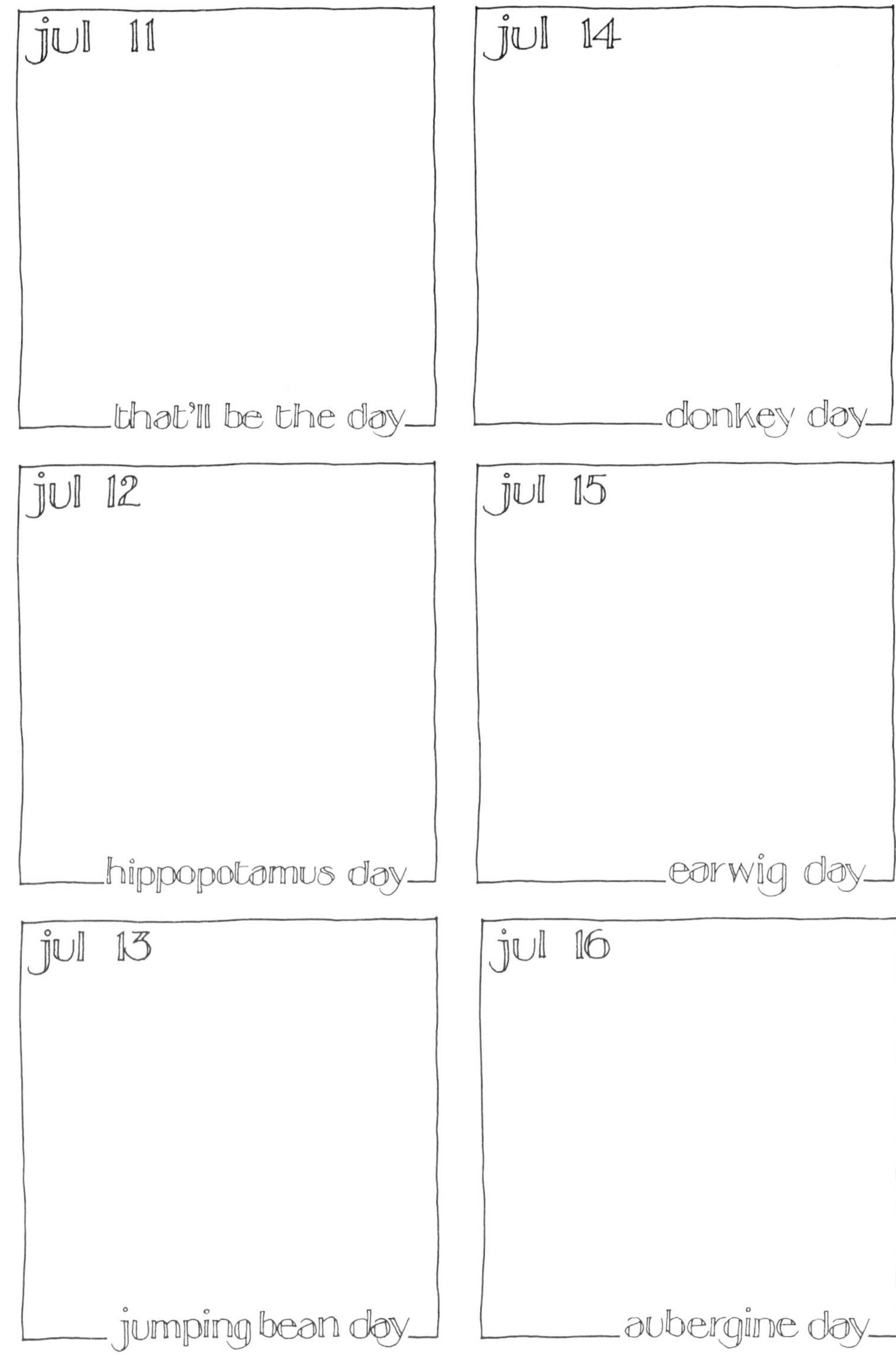

jul 11
that'll be the day
jul 12
hippopotamus day
jul 13
jumping bean day
jul 14
donkey day
jul 15
earwig day
jul 16
aubergine day

jul 17	jul 20
dodecahedron day	king day
jul 18	jul 21
dodo day	queen day
jul 19	jul 22
frankfurter day	knave day

LEO
(the lion) july 23 - aug 22

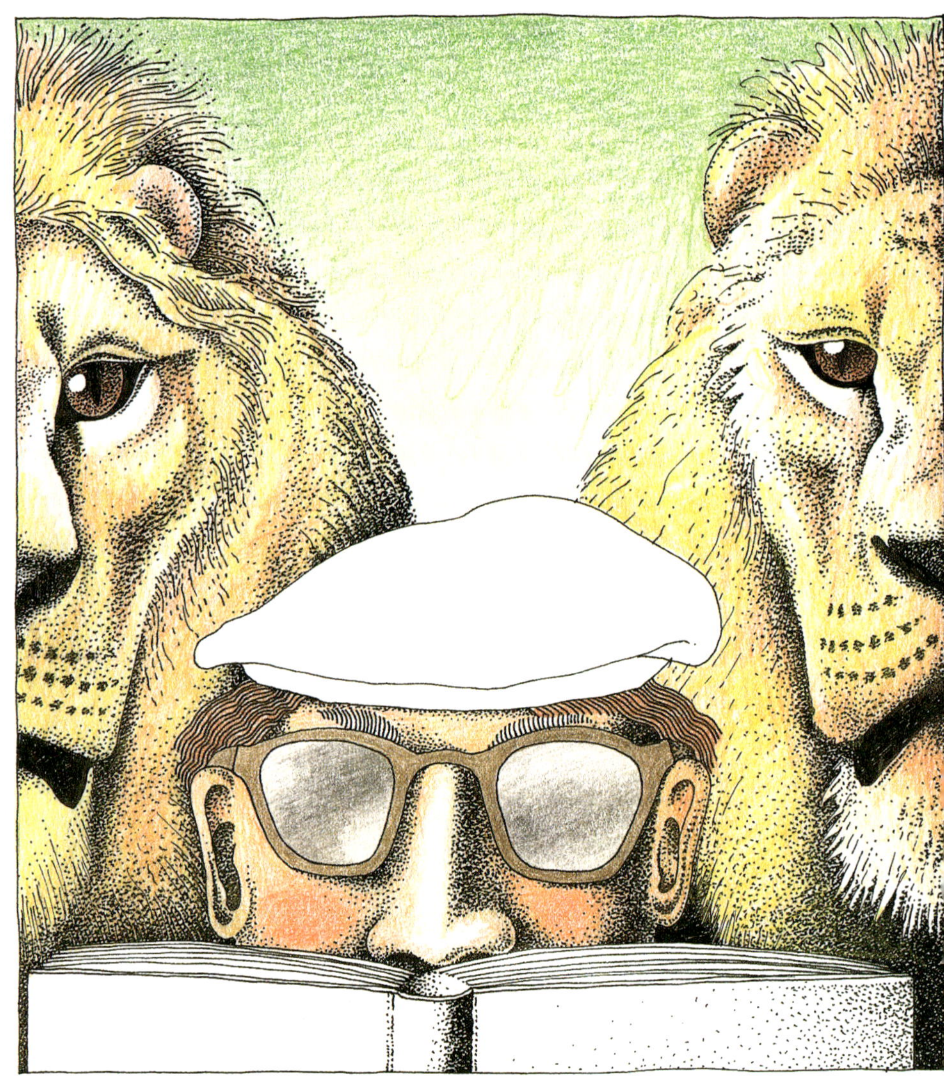

reading
between the lions

LEO

Those who are born underneath this great sign
are thoughtful, successful and certain to shine.
Betting temptations are easy to shun
unless there's a horse they want to see run,
then they profess that "this thing's a dead cert"
only to find that they soon lose their shirt.
In matters of food, they will eat to keep trim;
in matters of drink, they will stop at the brim.

jul 23

ace day

jul 24

dishcloth day

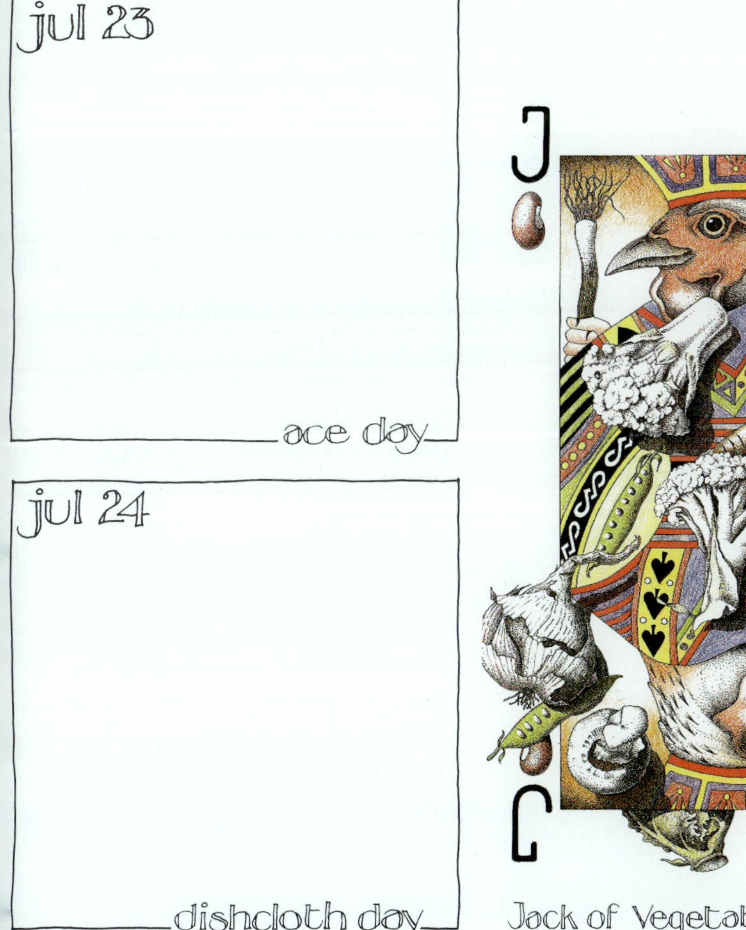

Jack of Vegetables

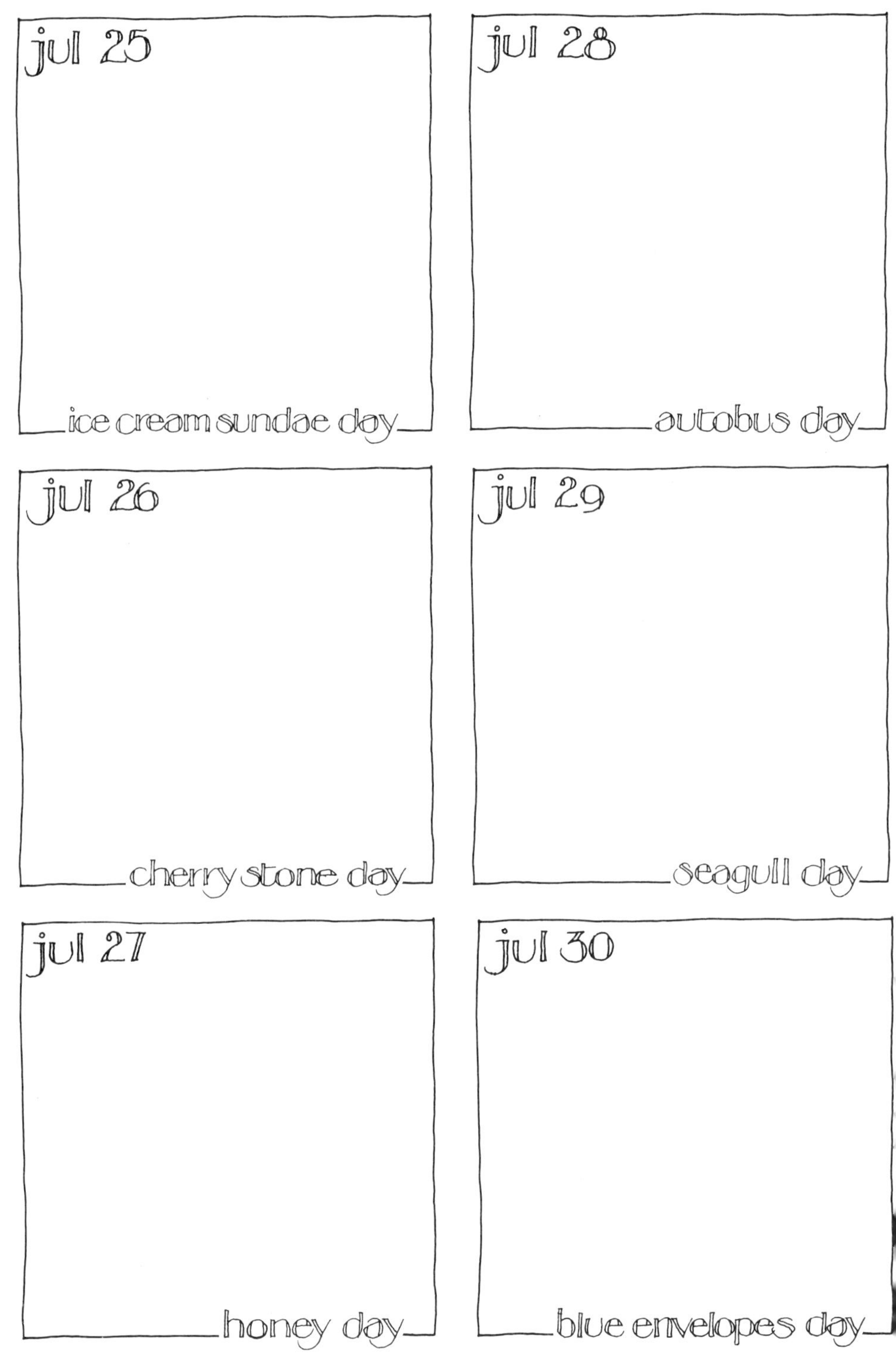
jul 25
ice cream sundae day

jul 26
cherry stone day

jul 27
honey day

jul 28
autobus day

jul 29
seagull day

jul 30
blue envelopes day

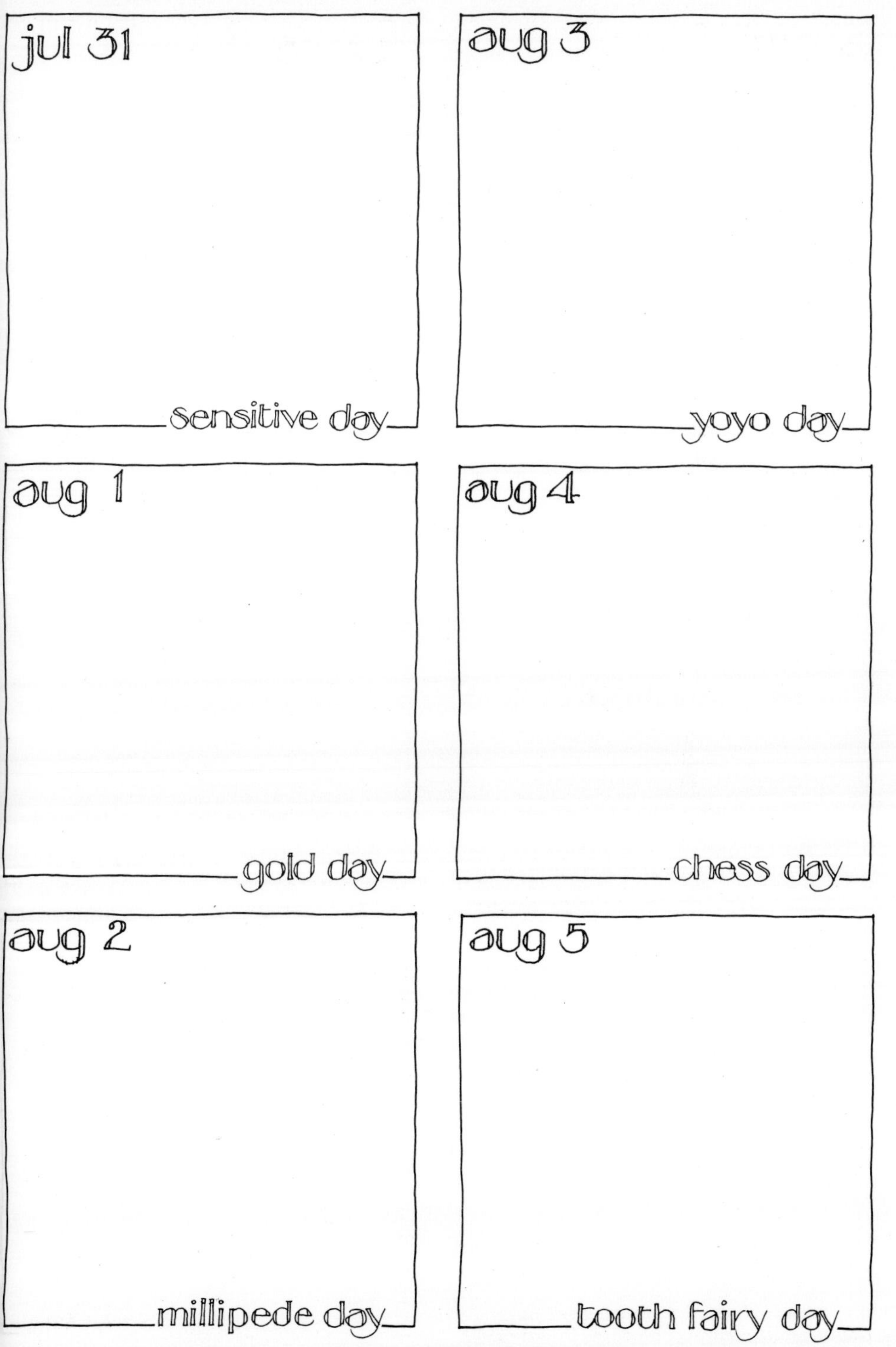

jul 31
sensitive day
aug 3
yoyo day
aug 1
gold day
aug 4
chess day
aug 2
millipede day
aug 5
tooth fairy day

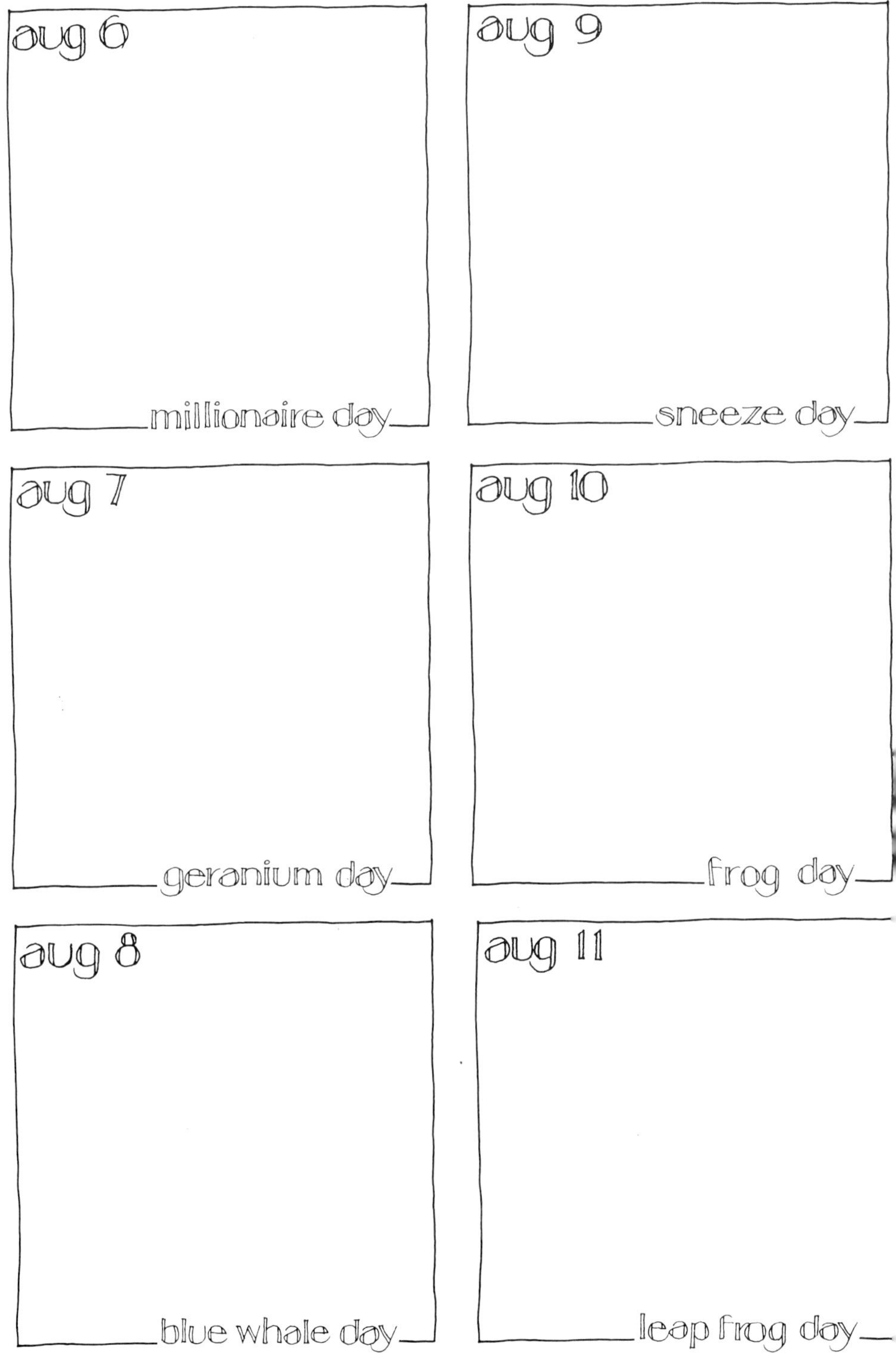

aug 6
millionaire day
aug 7
geranium day
aug 8
blue whale day
aug 9
sneeze day
aug 10
frog day
aug 11
leap frog day

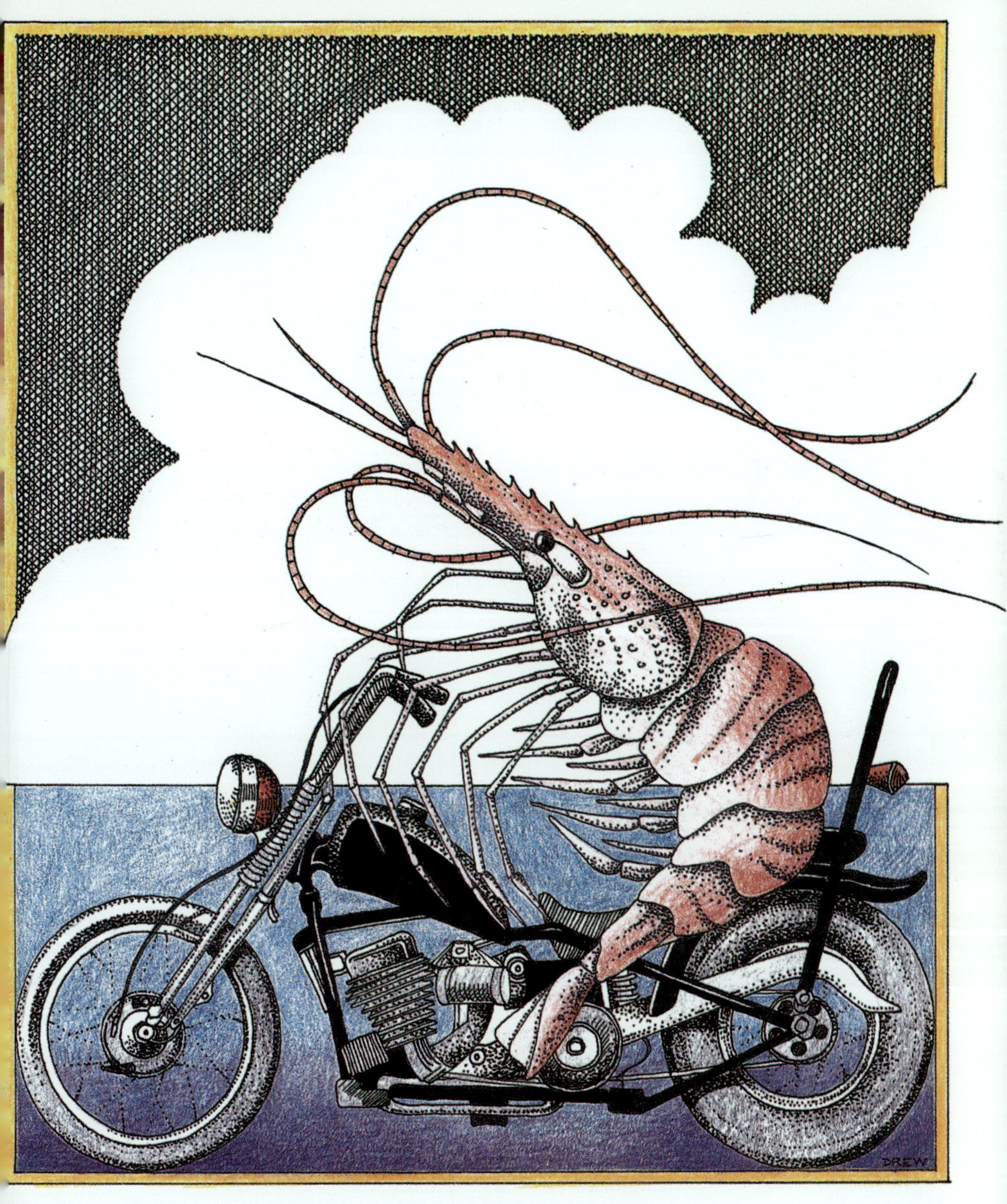

prawn to be wild

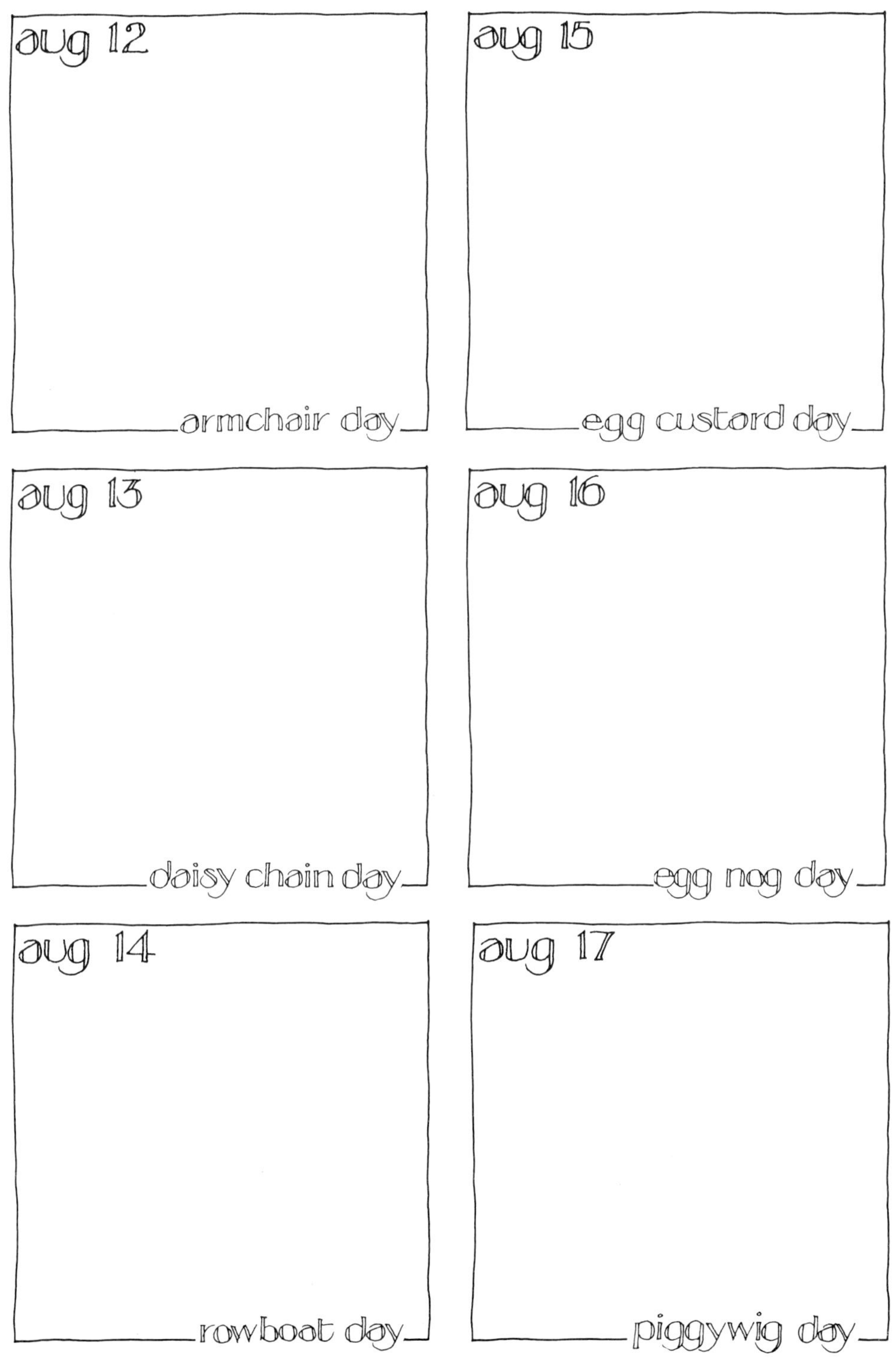

aug 12
armchair day
aug 13
daisy chain day
aug 14
rowboat day
aug 15
egg custard day
aug 16
egg nog day
aug 17
piggywig day

aug 18	aug 21
foxtrot day	rubber day

aug 19	
beethoven day	

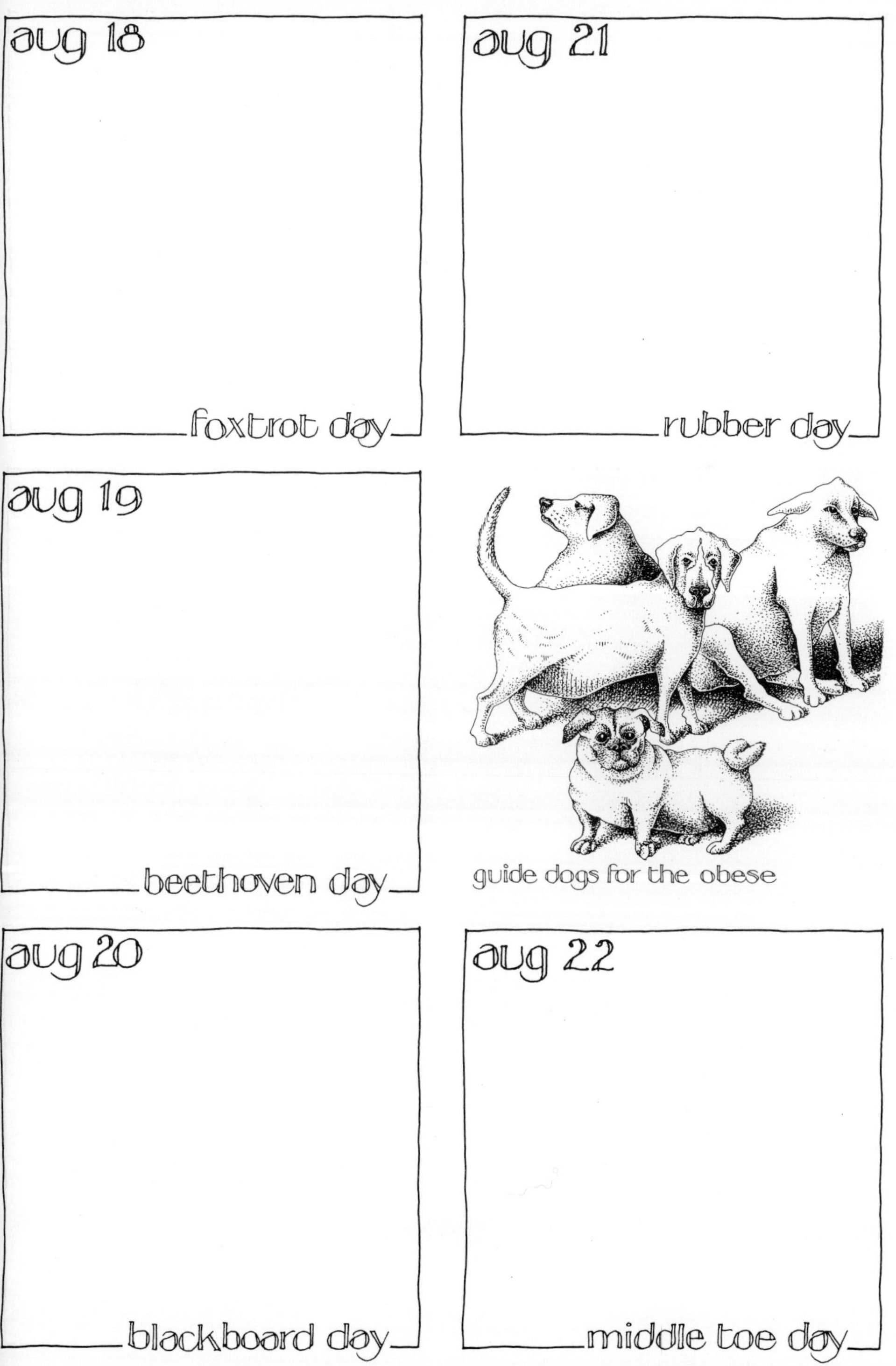

guide dogs for the obese

aug 20	aug 22
blackboard day	middle toe day

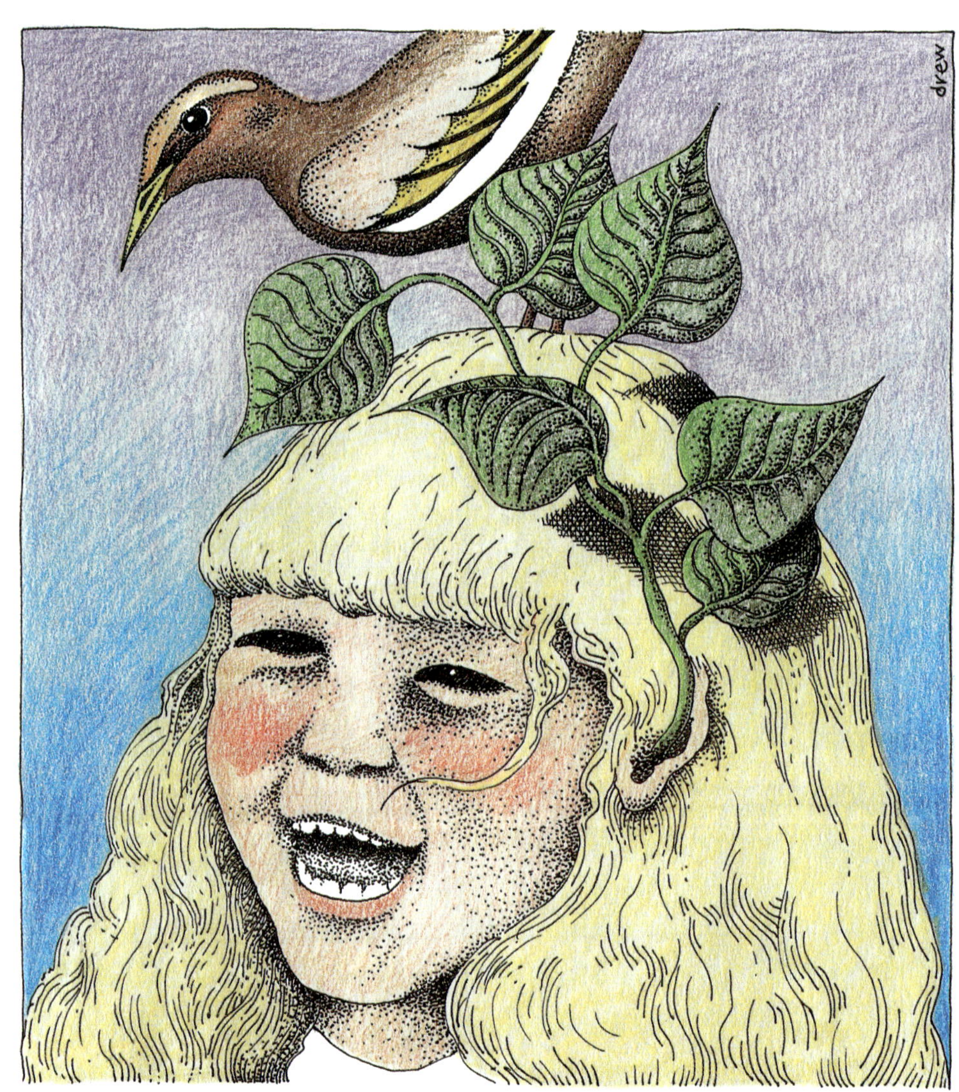

the virgin merry
(with virgin-ear creeper)

VIRGO

Those who are born underneath this great sign
are thoughtful, successful and certain to shine.
They usually limp but never in May;
they eat very little but offer to pay.
Their worst inclination is not often seen:
they burst into tears singing God Save the
Queen.

And if there's a habit they try not to show
it's keeping a peanut between every toe.

aug 23

aug 24

mistletoe day

mistle thrush day

grets
've had a few,
ut then
gain ...)

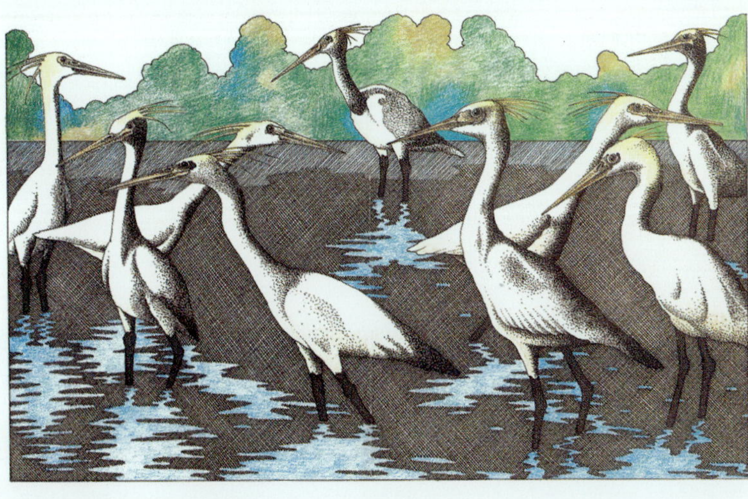

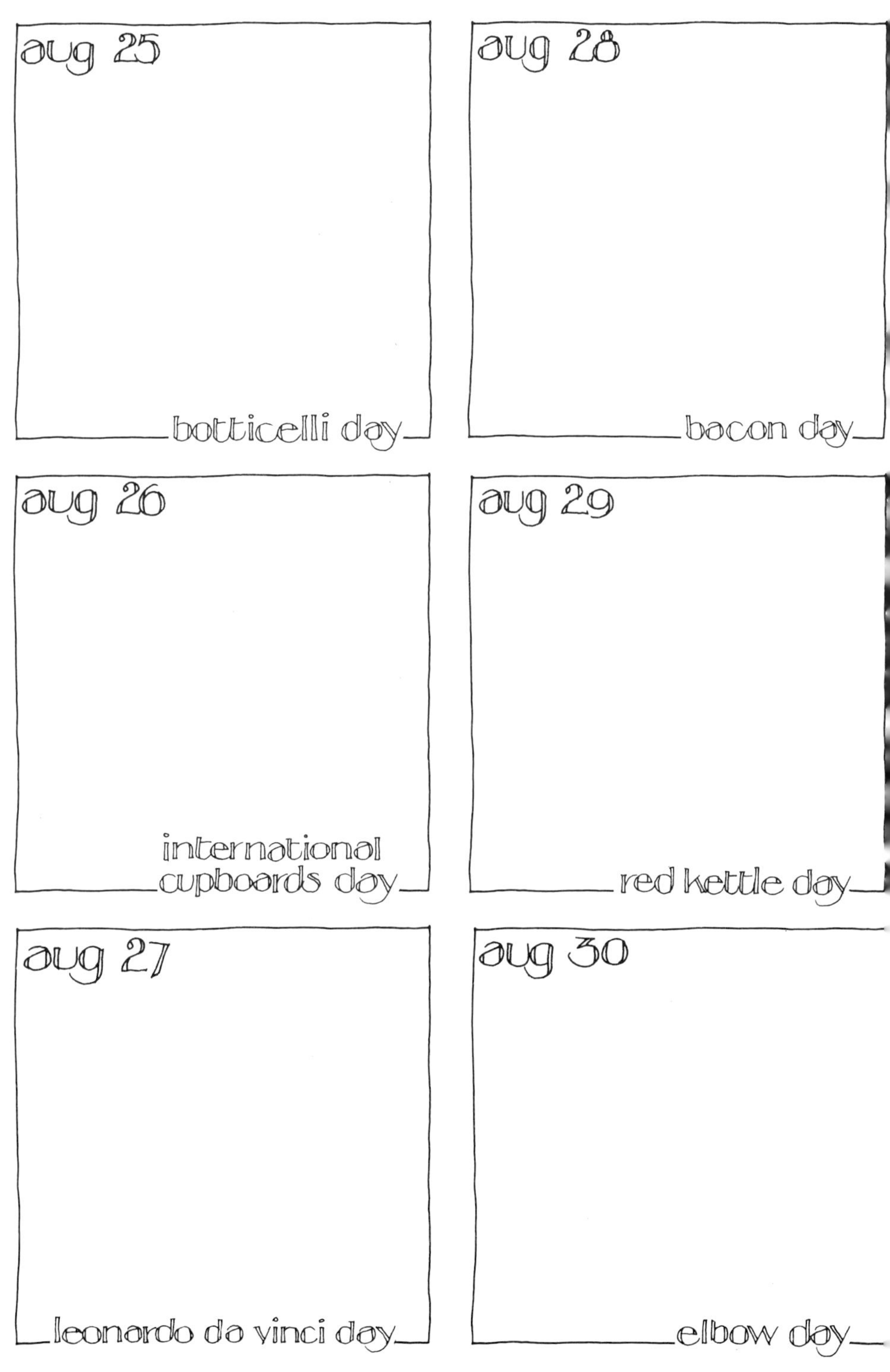
aug 25
botticelli day
aug 26
international
cupboards day
aug 27
leonardo da vinci day
aug 28
bacon day
aug 29
red kettle day
aug 30
elbow day

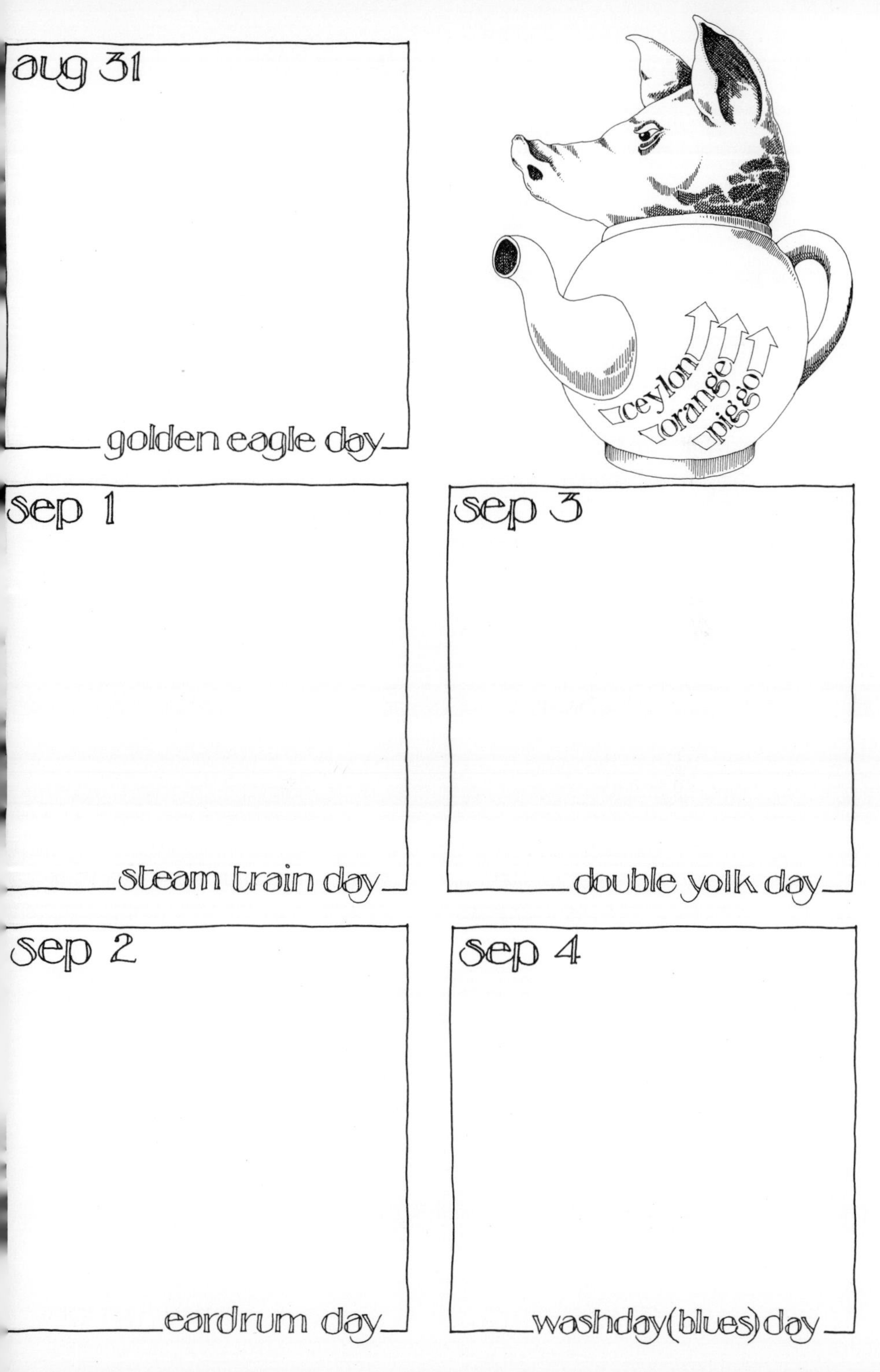

aug 31

golden eagle day

sep 1

steam train day

sep 2

eardrum day

sep 3

double yolk day

sep 4

washday (blues) day

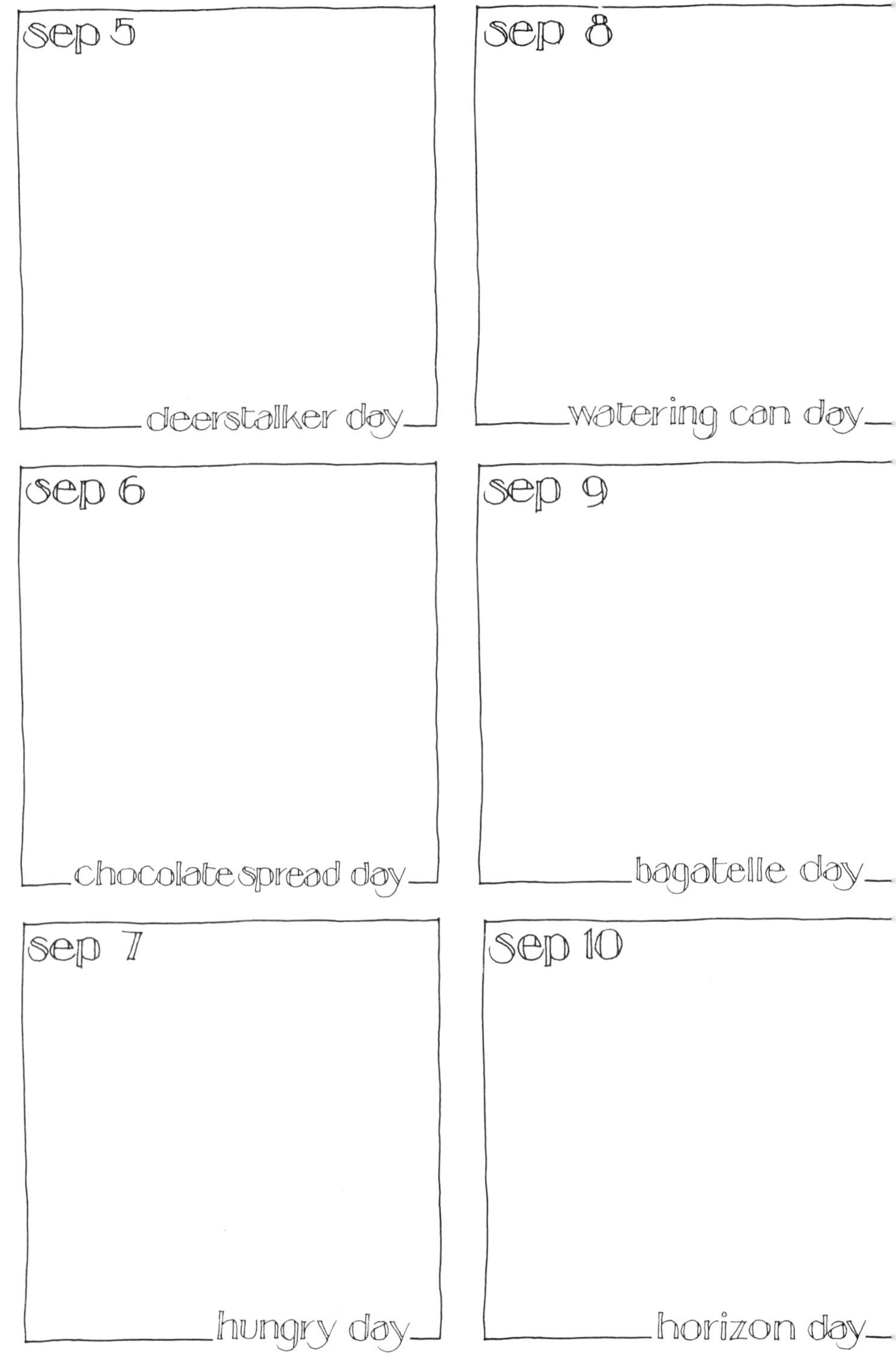

sep 5
deerstalker day

sep 8
watering can day

sep 6
chocolate spread day

sep 9
bagatelle day

sep 7
hungry day

sep 10
horizon day

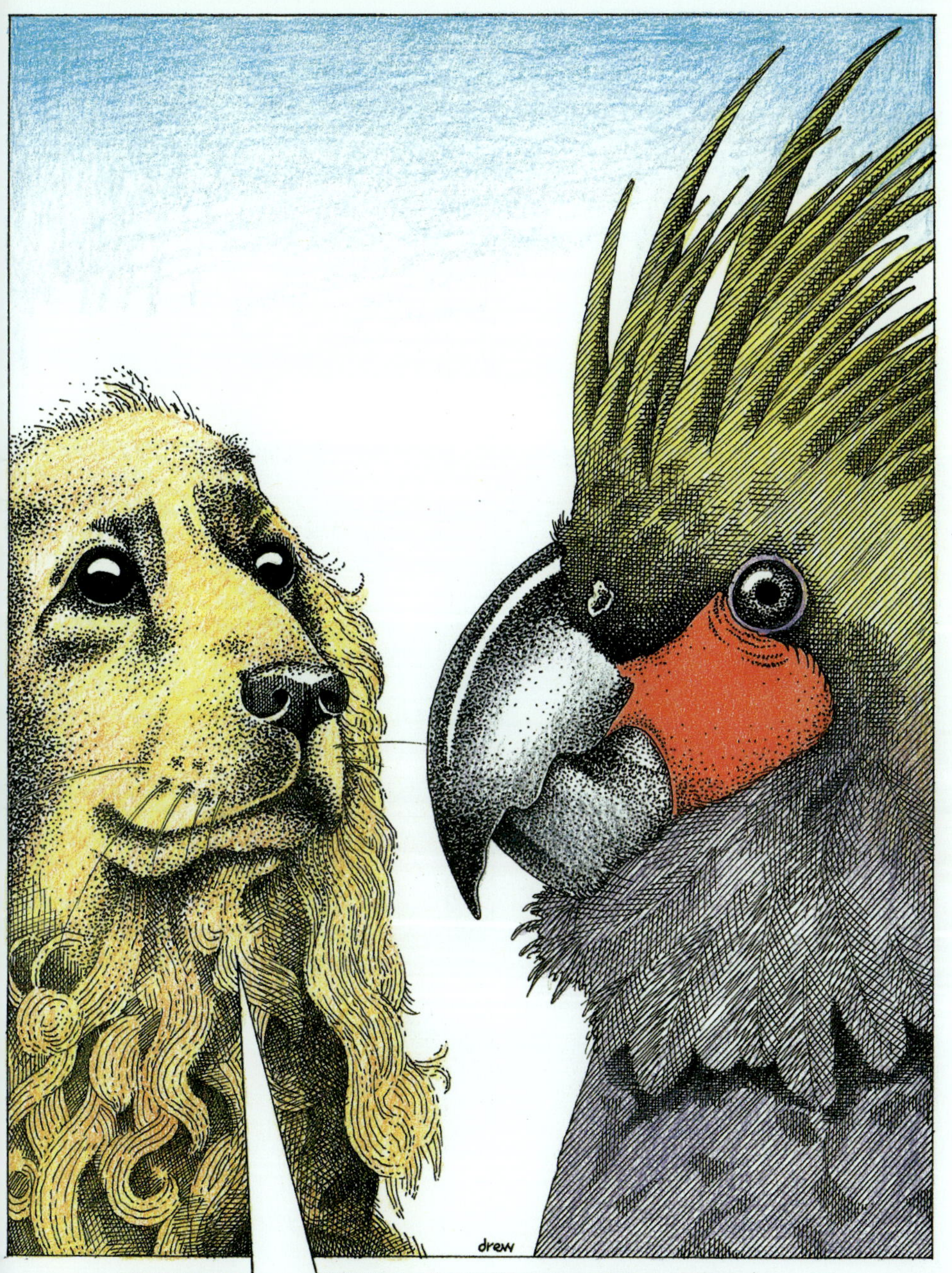
are you a cocker, too?

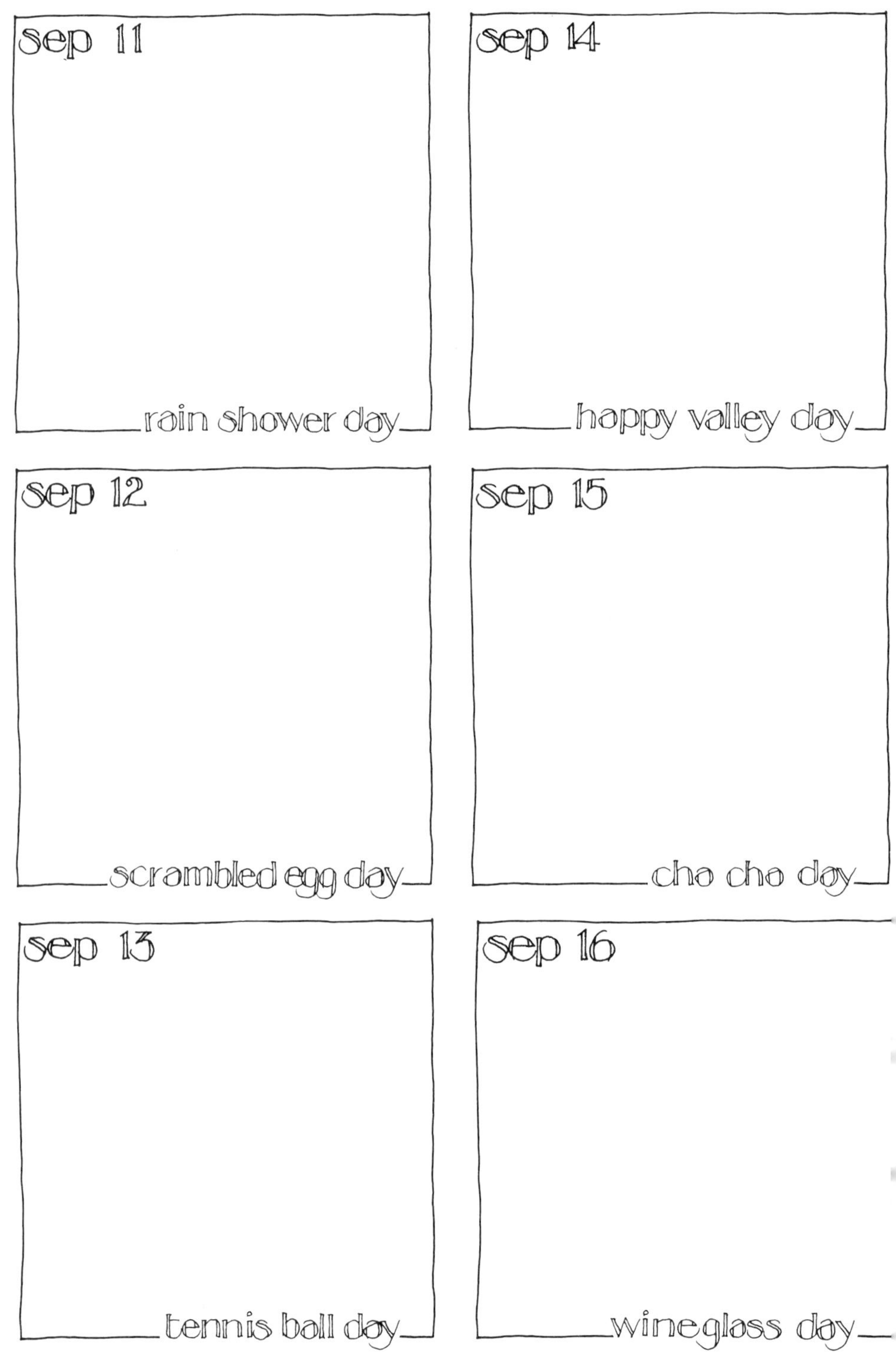

sep 11
rain shower day
sep 12
scrambled egg day
sep 13
tennis ball day
sep 14
happy valley day
sep 15
cha cha day
sep 16
wineglass day

sep 17	sep 20
honey bee day	ice cream day
sep 18	sep 21
binocular day	toffee day
sep 19	sep 22
doo dah doo dah day	pot of gold day

LIBRA
(the balance) sept 23 to oct 23

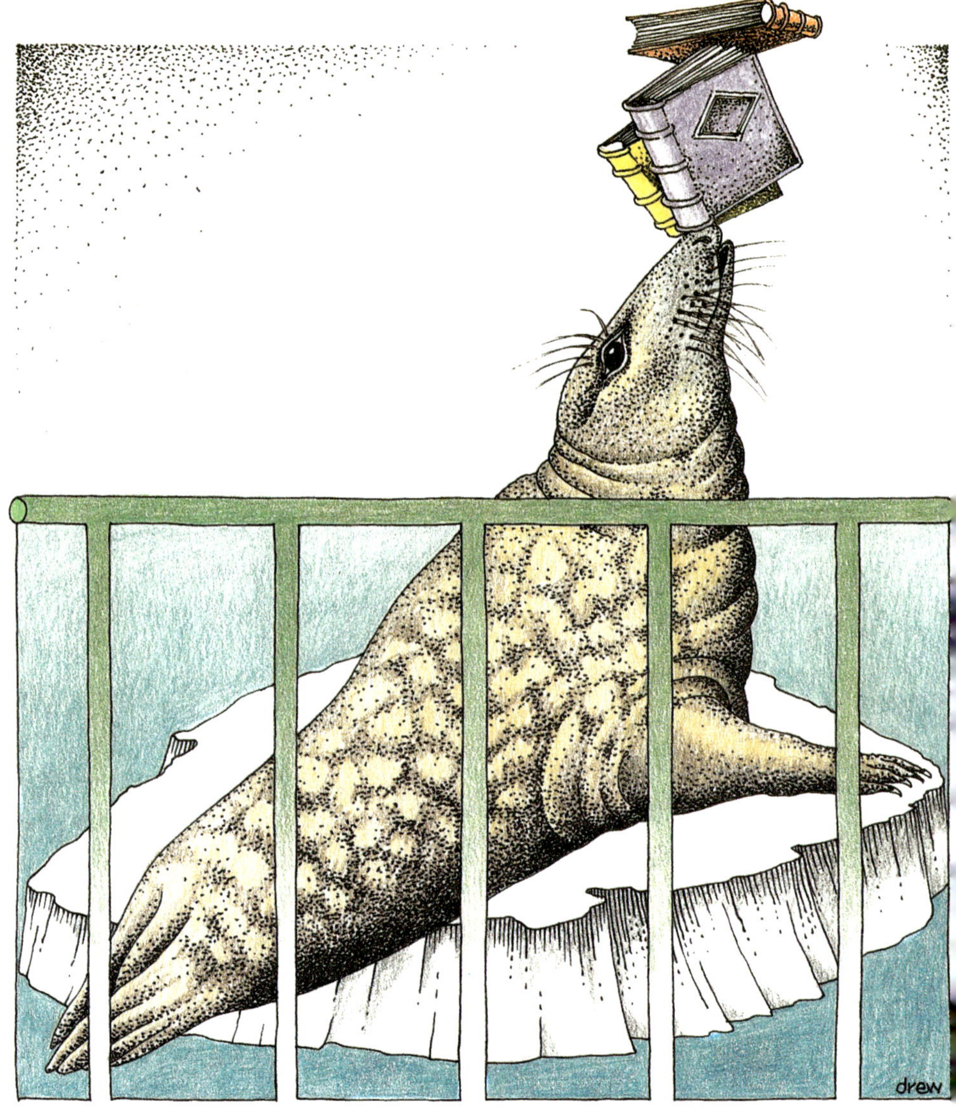

drew

balancing
the books

LIBRA
Those who are born underneath this great sign
are thoughtful, successful and certain to shine.
They never refuse to take trips on a train;
they say they're related to Abel not Cain.
And when an old donkey can yodel and bray
they say that they taught it the previous day.
It's not that I'm saying they lie in this way
but can you believe that they heard Mozart
play?

sep 23

_____ trombone day_____

sep 25

_____ church bells day_____

sep 24

_____ dog and bone day_____

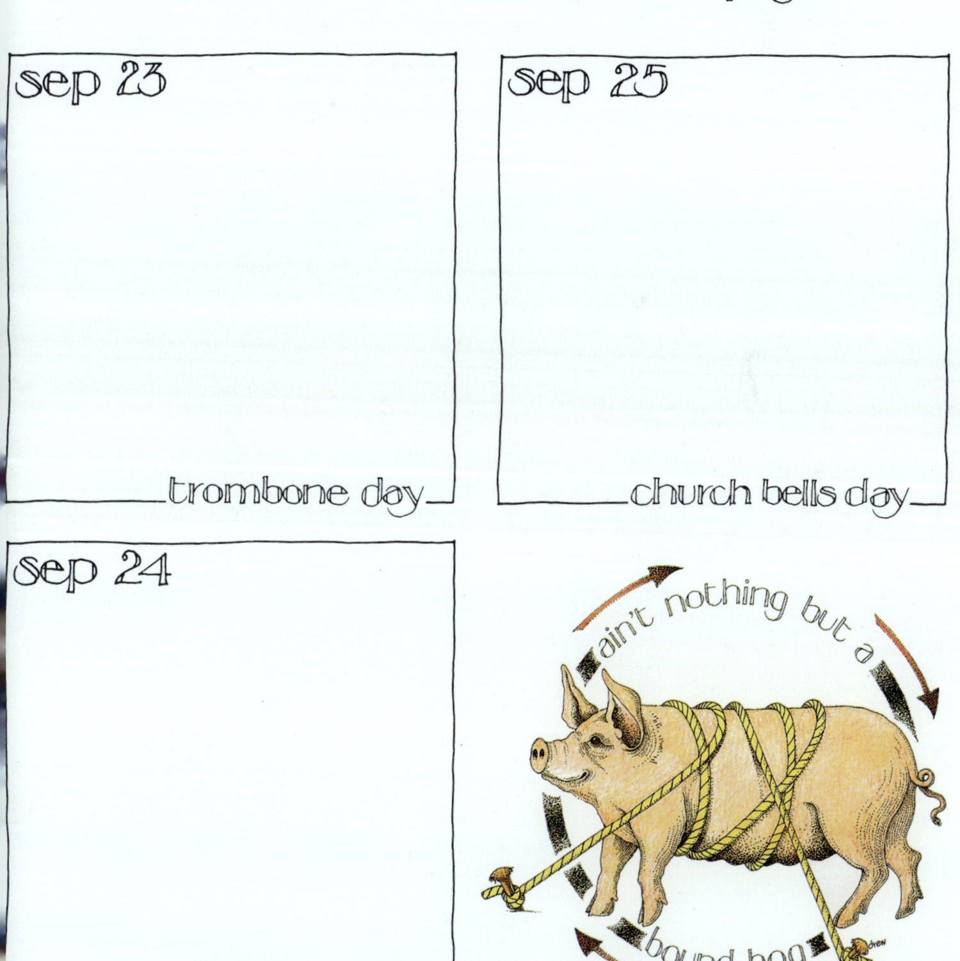

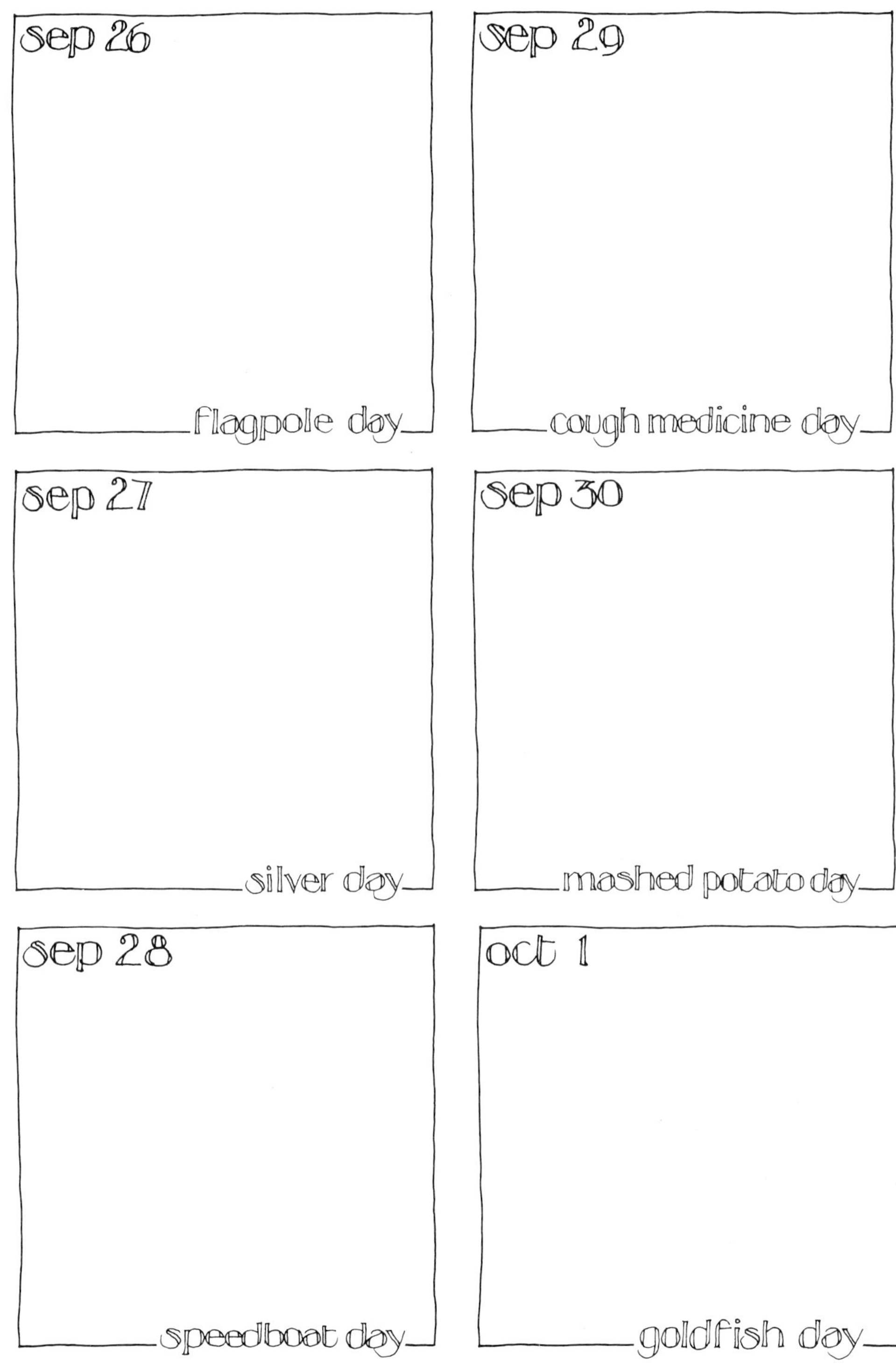

sep 26
flagpole day
sep 27
silver day
sep 28
speedboat day
sep 29
cough medicine day
sep 30
mashed potato day
oct 1
goldfish day

oct 2	oct 4
wise owl day	_sweet potato day_
oct 3	oct 5
daffodil day	_dustbin day_

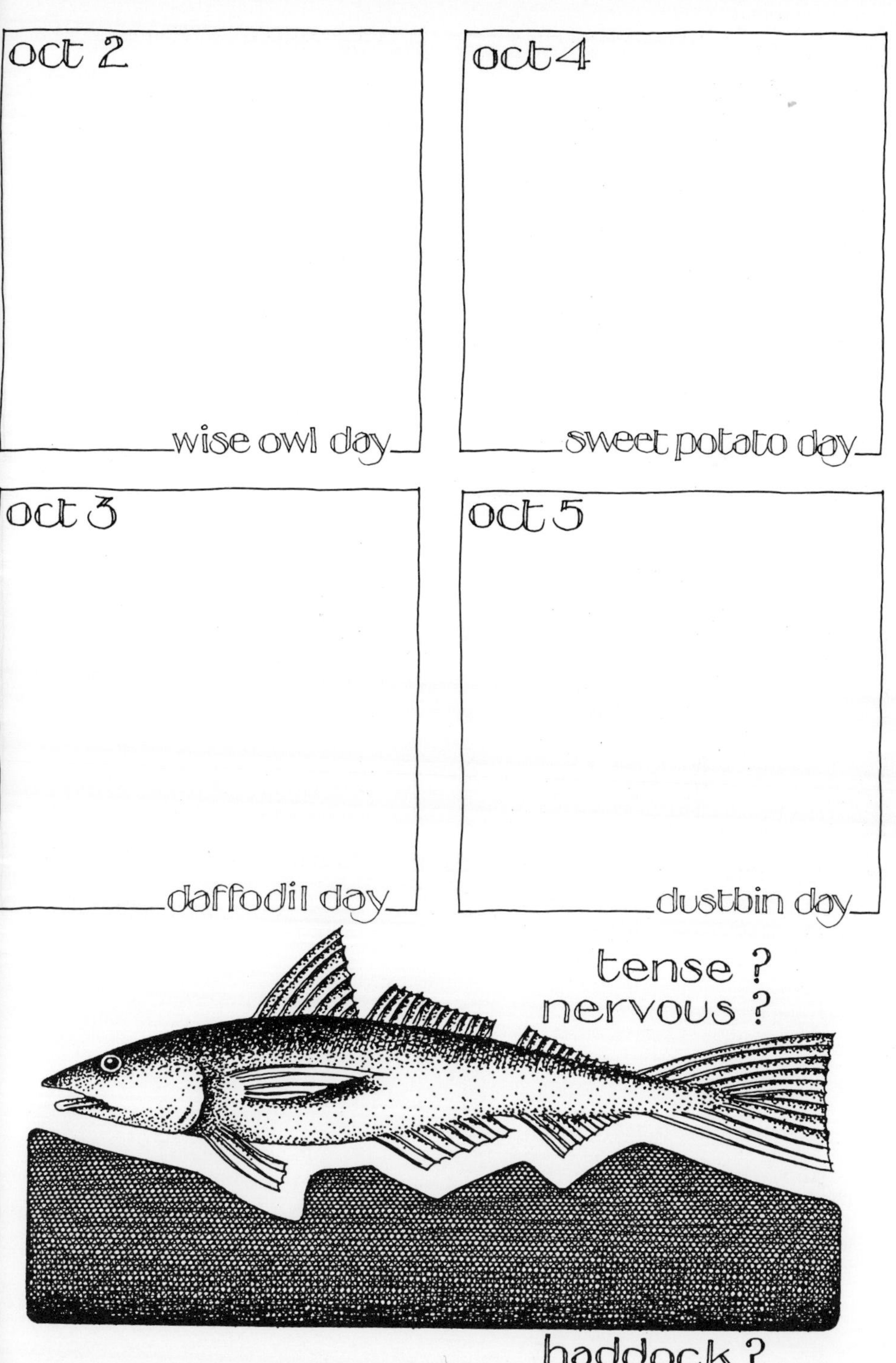

oct 6

_______designer day_

oct 8

_______little dog day_

oct 7

_______funfair day_

oct 9

_______hot sausage day_

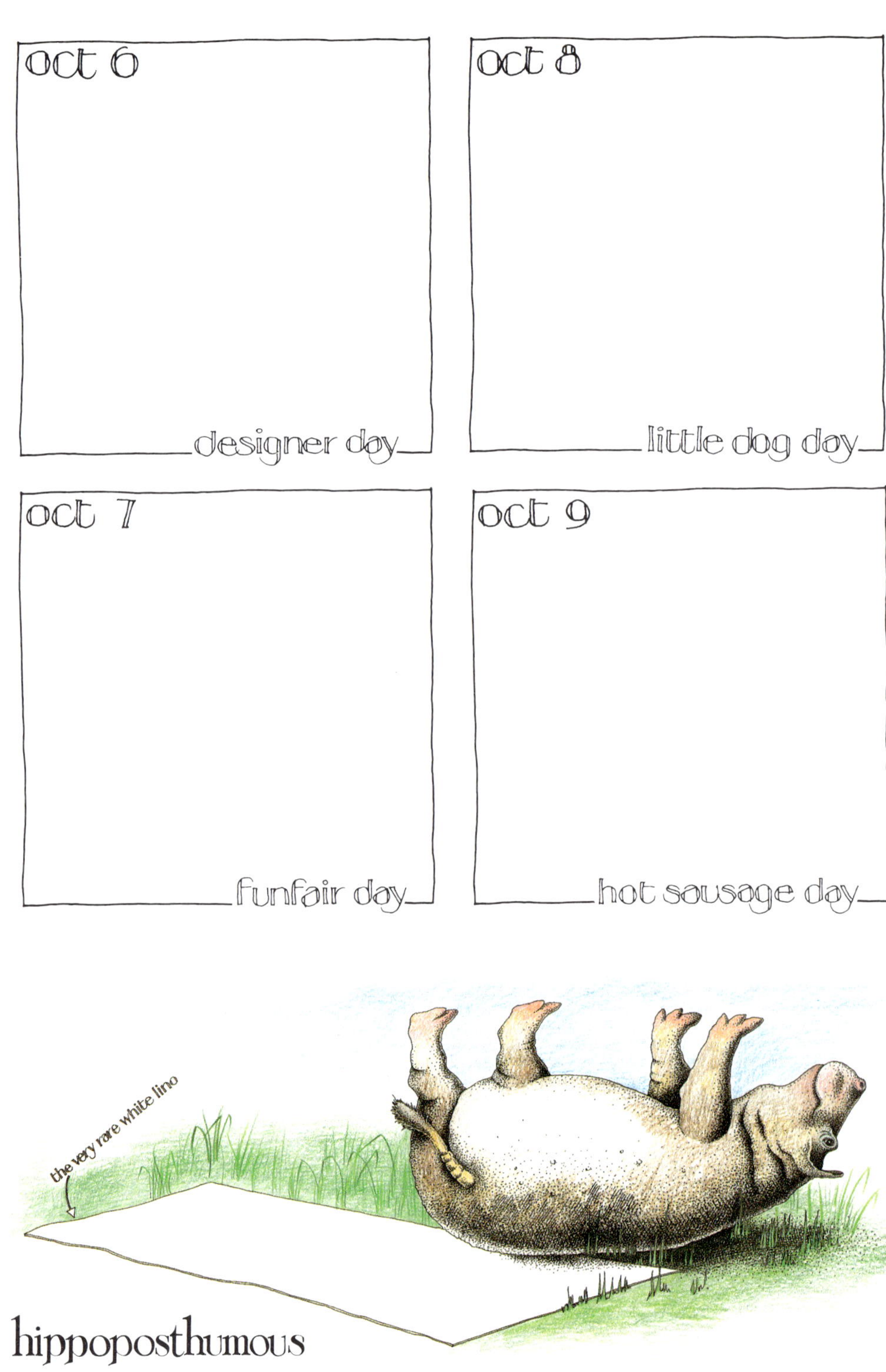

hippoposthumous

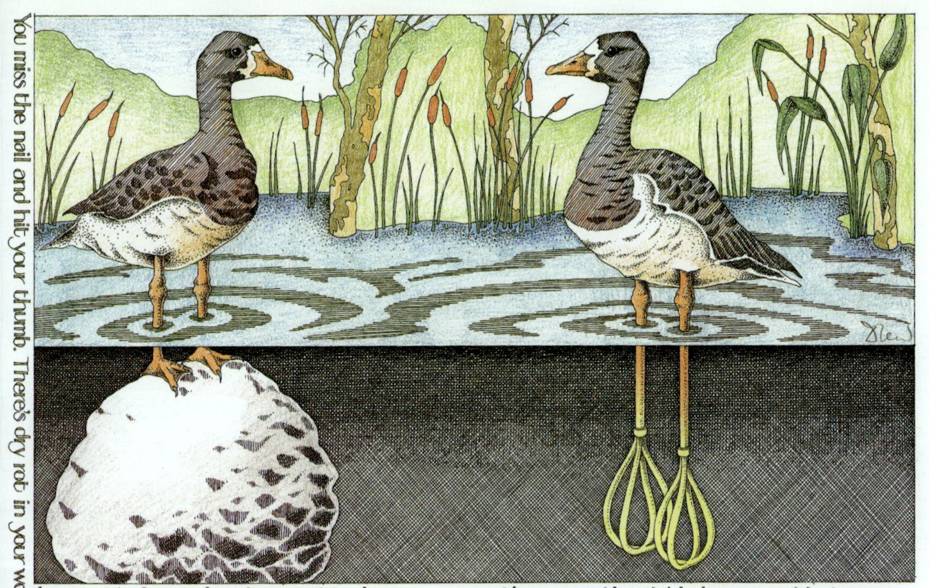

<table>
<tr><td>oct 10

white cow day</td><td>oct 11

cold tap day</td></tr>
</table>

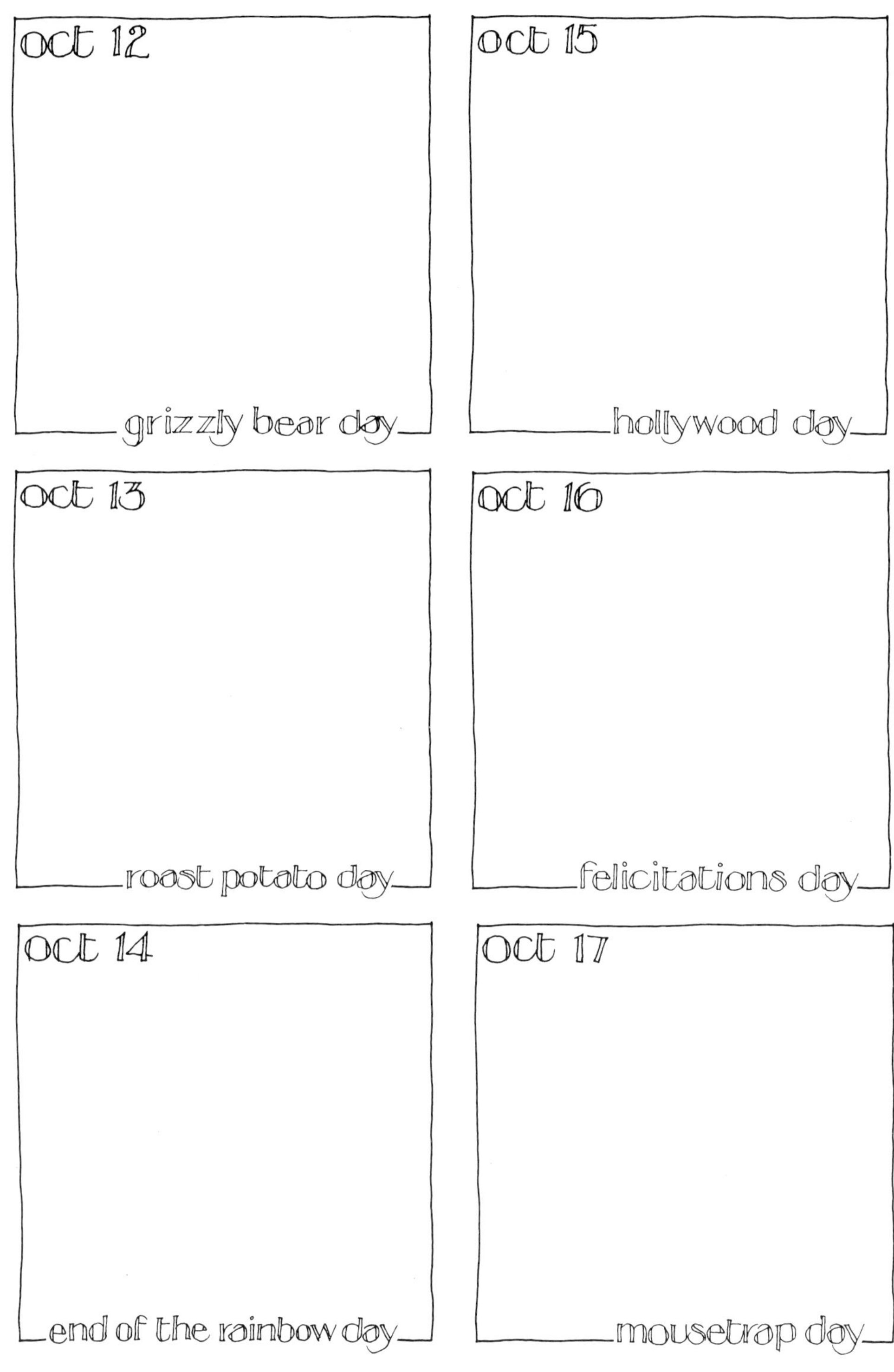

oct 12
grizzly bear day

oct 13
roast potato day

oct 14
end of the rainbow day

oct 15
hollywood day

oct 16
felicitations day

oct 17
mousetrap day

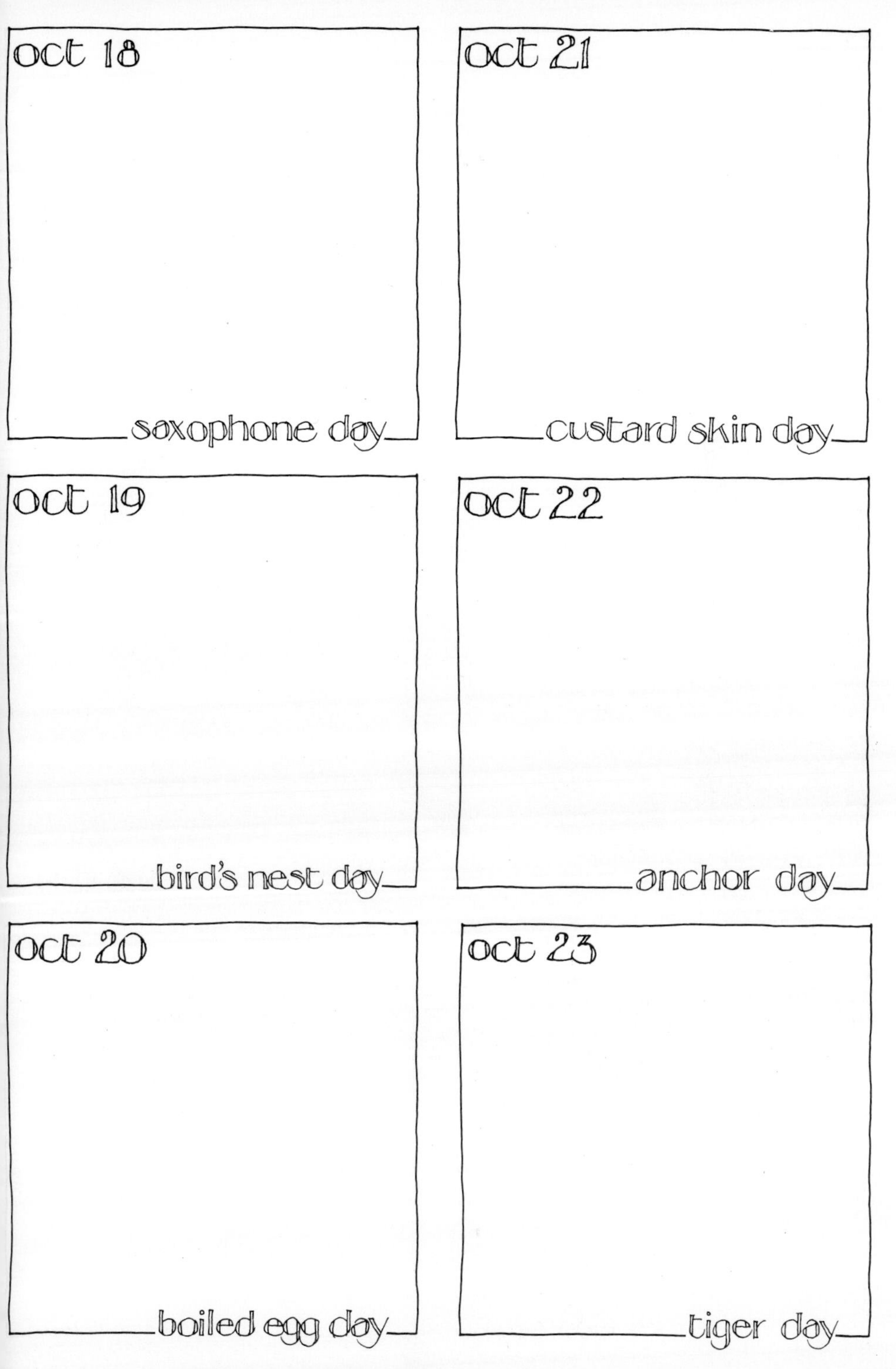

oct 18
saxophone day

oct 21
custard skin day

oct 19
bird's nest day

oct 22
anchor day

oct 20
boiled egg day

oct 23
tiger day

SCORPIO
(the scorpion) oct 24 to nov 21

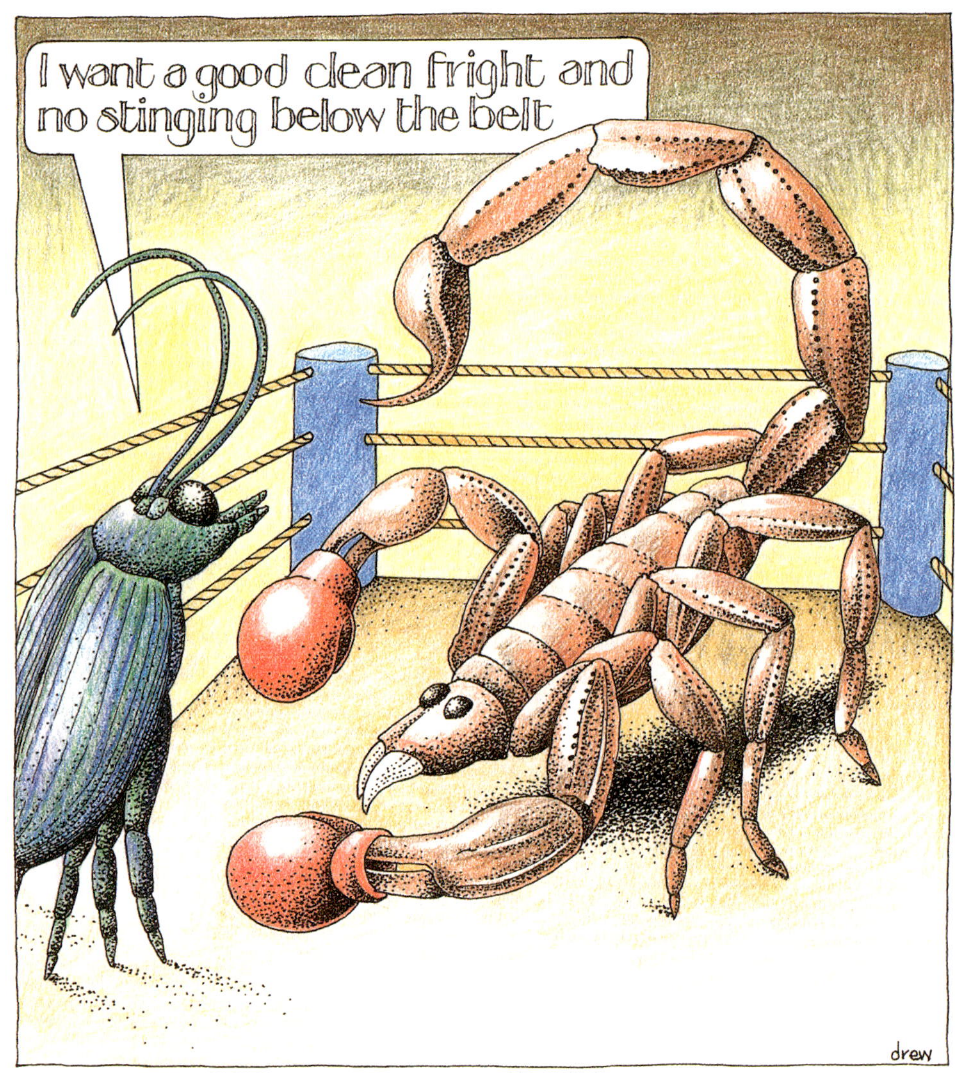

heavyweight scorpion of the world

SCORPIO

Those who are born underneath this great sign
are thoughtful, successful and certain to shine.
They polish their shoes till they gleam in the sun,
they love to play chess and they shriek when
they've won.

When they get old they will talk of the past
and how each decade is not like the last
and food of today "is so poor on the whole"
but give them potatoes, they eat the
whole bowl.

oct 24

computer day

oct 25

sailaway day

Two all....
('n tents
and porpoises)

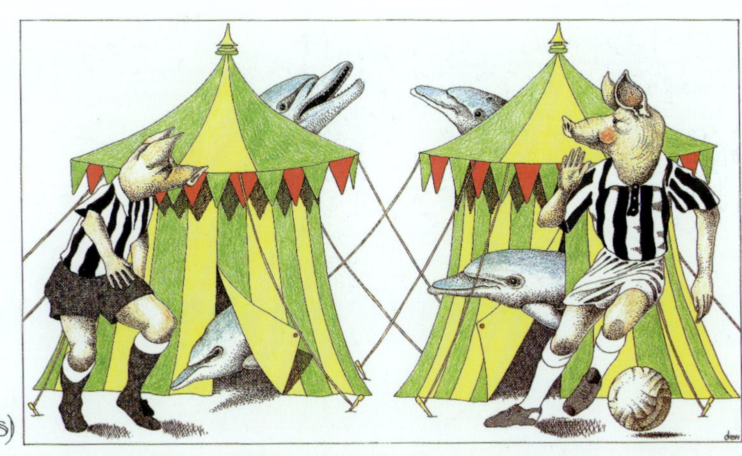

oct 26

sweet chestnut day

oct 27

zebra day

oct 28

plughole day

oct 29

pluto day

oct 30

slow waltz day

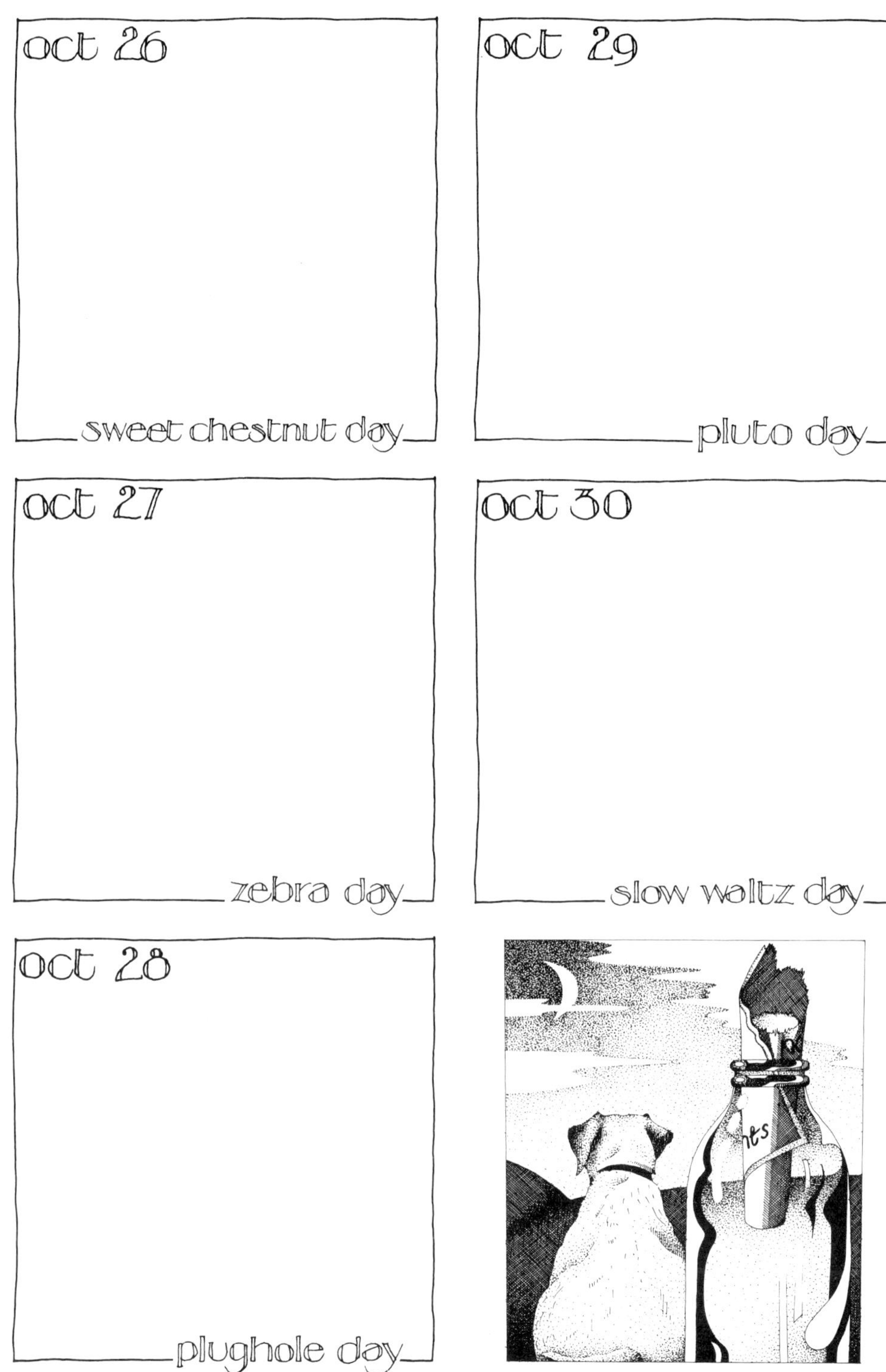

<table>
<tr><td>

oct 31

electricity day
</td><td>

nov 3

chocolate biscuits day
</td></tr>
<tr><td>

nov 1

big toe day
</td><td>

nov 4

tadpole day
</td></tr>
<tr><td>

nov 2

fresh fish day
</td><td>

nov 5

forks day
</td></tr>
</table>

nov 6

nov 7

nov 8

nov 9

nov 10

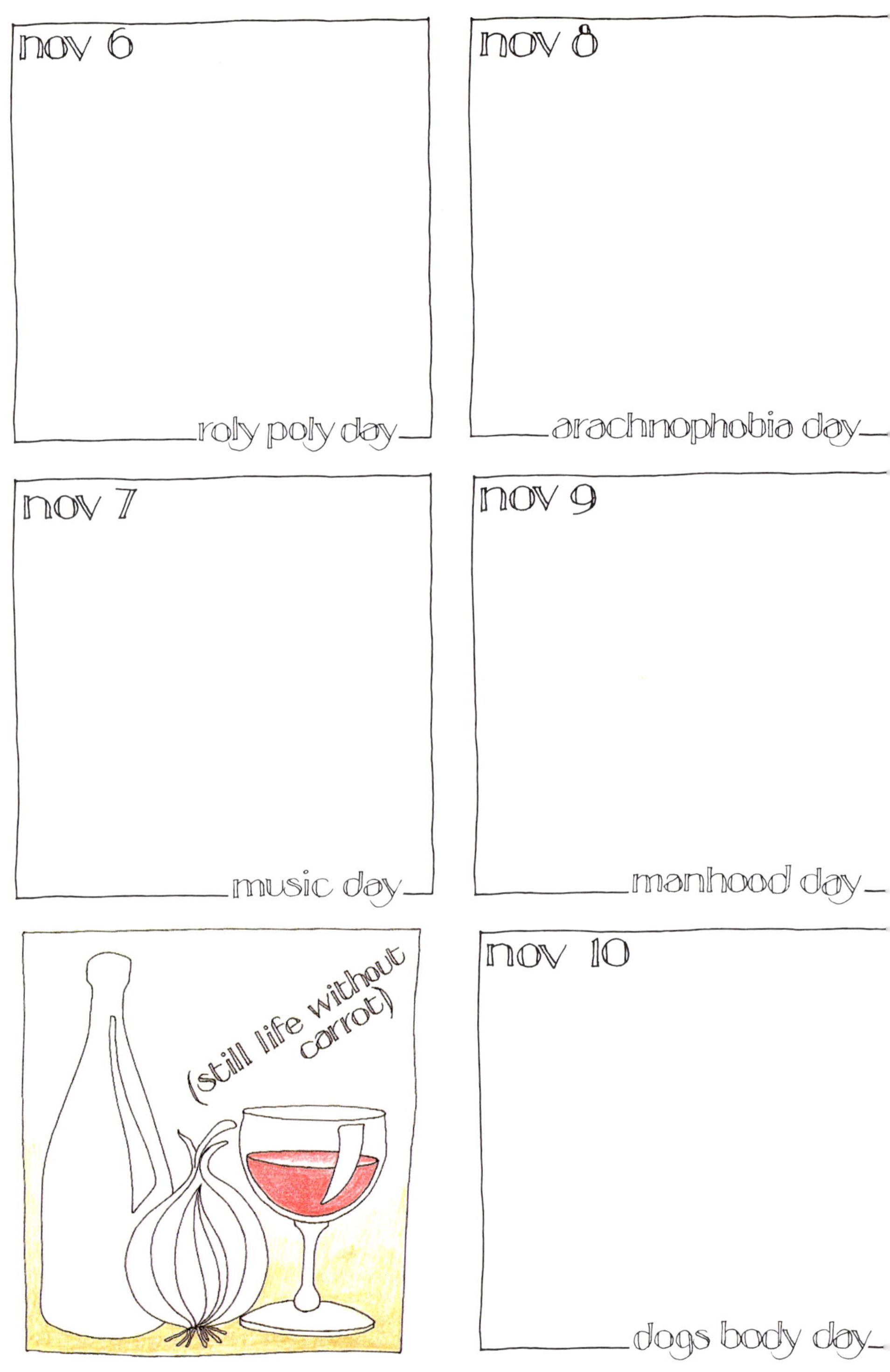

the lobster family: 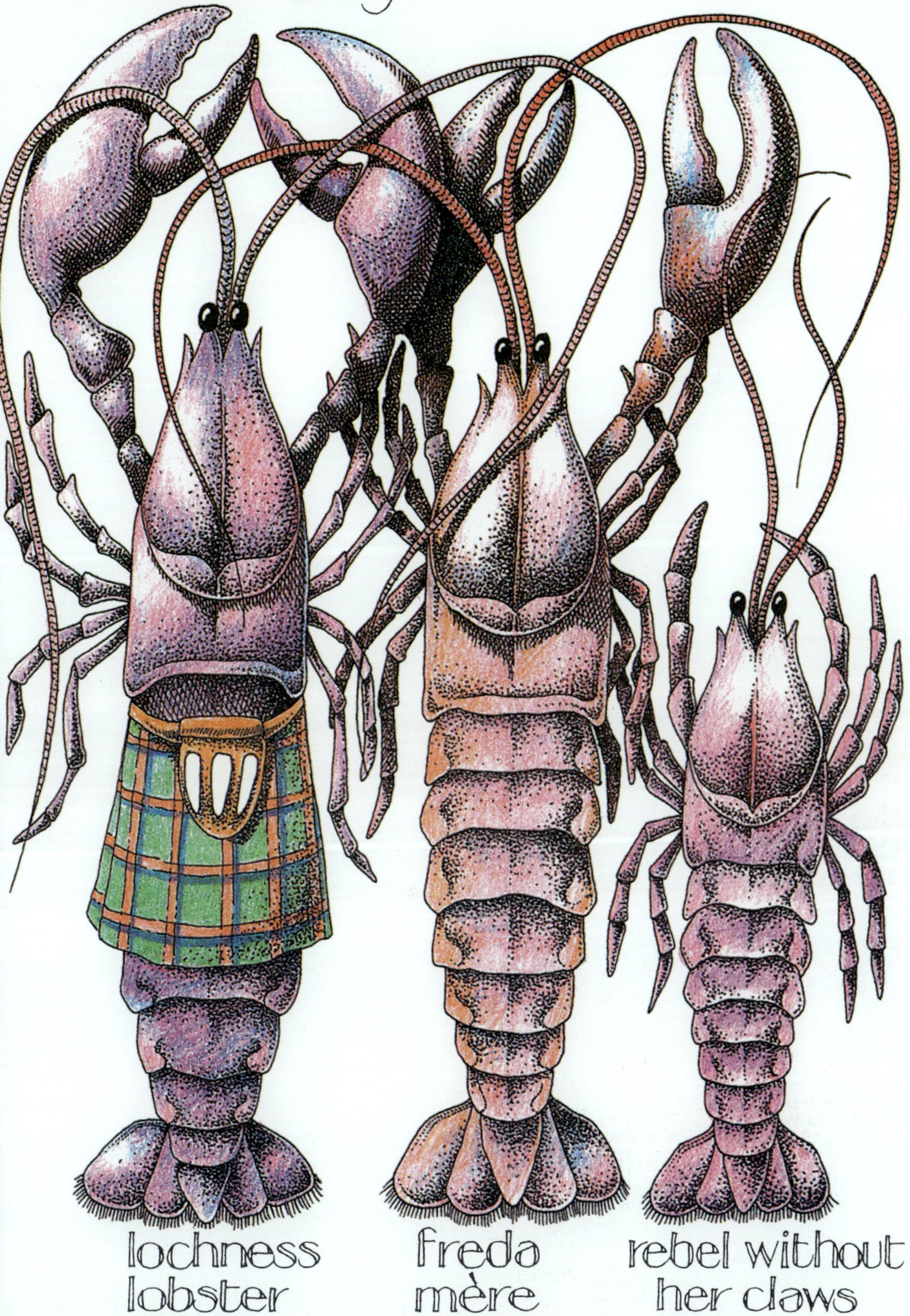
lochness
lobster
freda
mère
rebel without
her claws

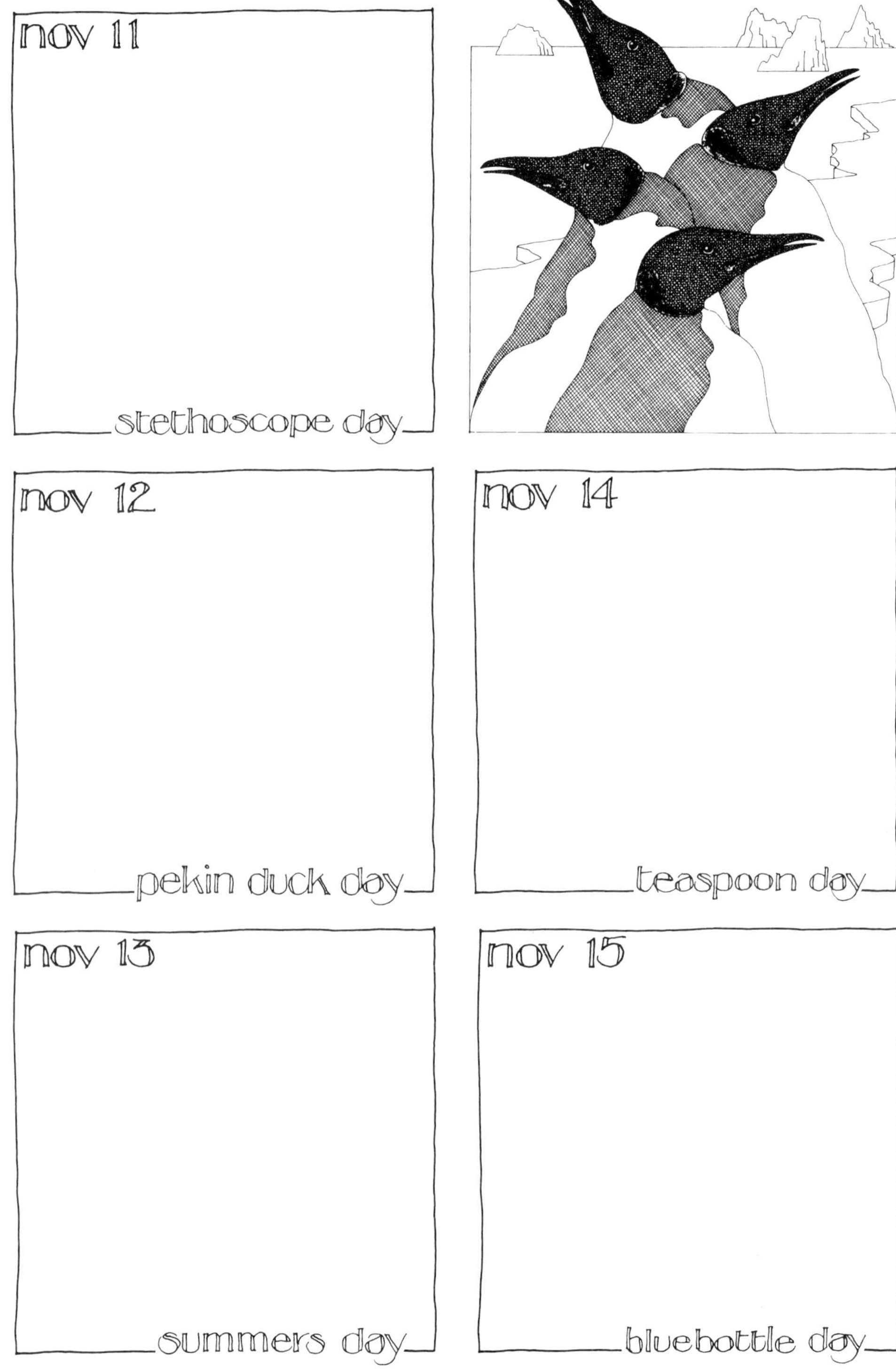

nov 11

stethoscope day

nov 12

pekin duck day

nov 13

summers day

nov 14

teaspoon day

nov 15

bluebottle day

nov 16	nov 19
can opener day	beachcomber day
nov 17	nov 20
eye opener day	bath tub day
nov 18	nov 21
hairpin day	red carnation day

SAGITTARIUS
(the archer) nov 22 to dec 21

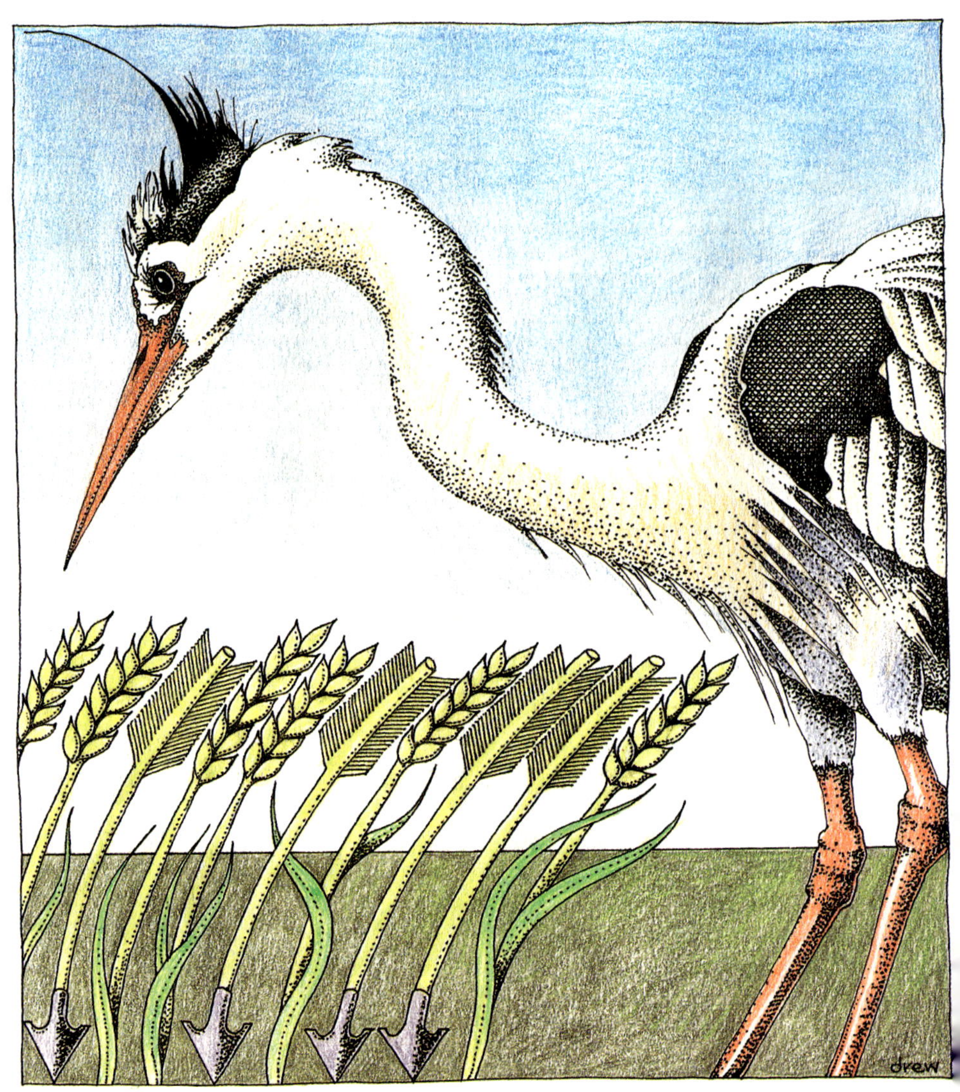

arrows by any other name
would smell as wheat

SAGITTARIUS

Those who are born underneath this great sign
are thoughtful, successful and certain to shine.
They have quite a passion for launching
large ships.
They'll only eat cabbage if cut into strips.
They often grow hair that they twist into
plaits
and hide it away under black bowler hats.
Their teeth are like granite with edges of steel;
they sound like machinery during a meal.

nov 22

____ fossil day ____

nov 24

____ rock and roll day ____

nov 23

____ incubator day ____

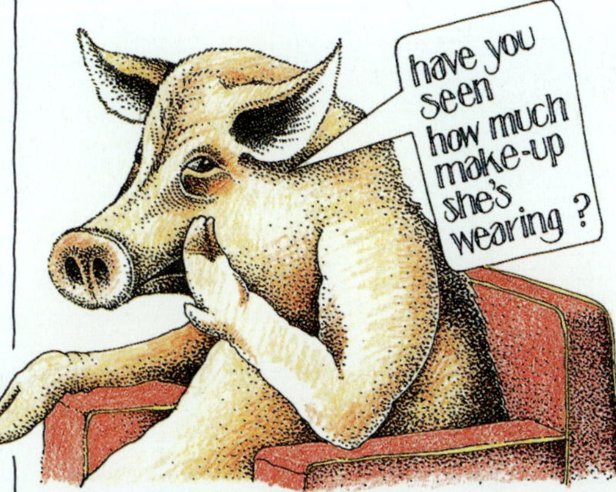

aside of bacon

| nov 25

green pea day | nov 27

raisin day |
| nov 26

green bean day | nov 28

peanut day |

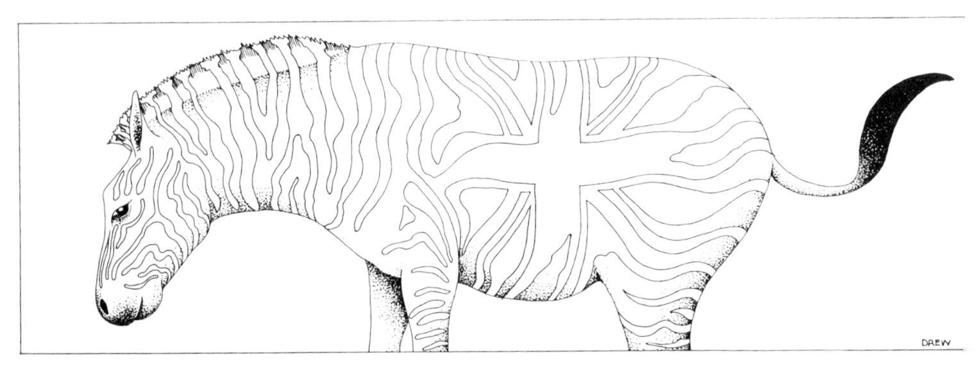

nov 29

_______________ torch day___

nov 30

_______ candle wax day___

dec 1

_______ peacock day___

dec 2

_______ hole in one day___

dec 3

_______ brandy snap day___

dec 4

_______ bank manager day___

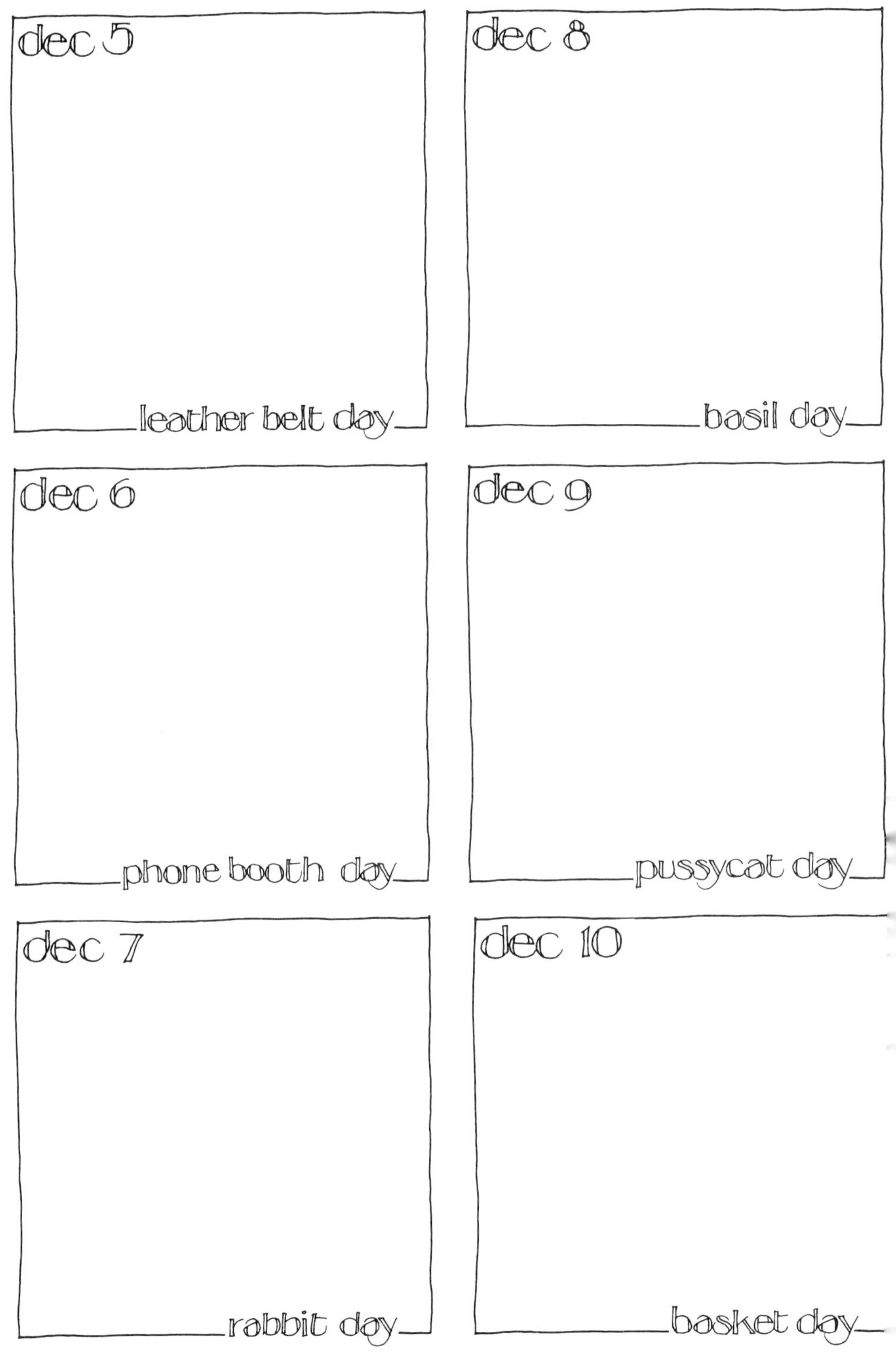
dec 5
leather belt day

dec 6
phone booth day

dec 7
rabbit day

dec 8
basil day

dec 9
pussycat day

dec 10
basket day

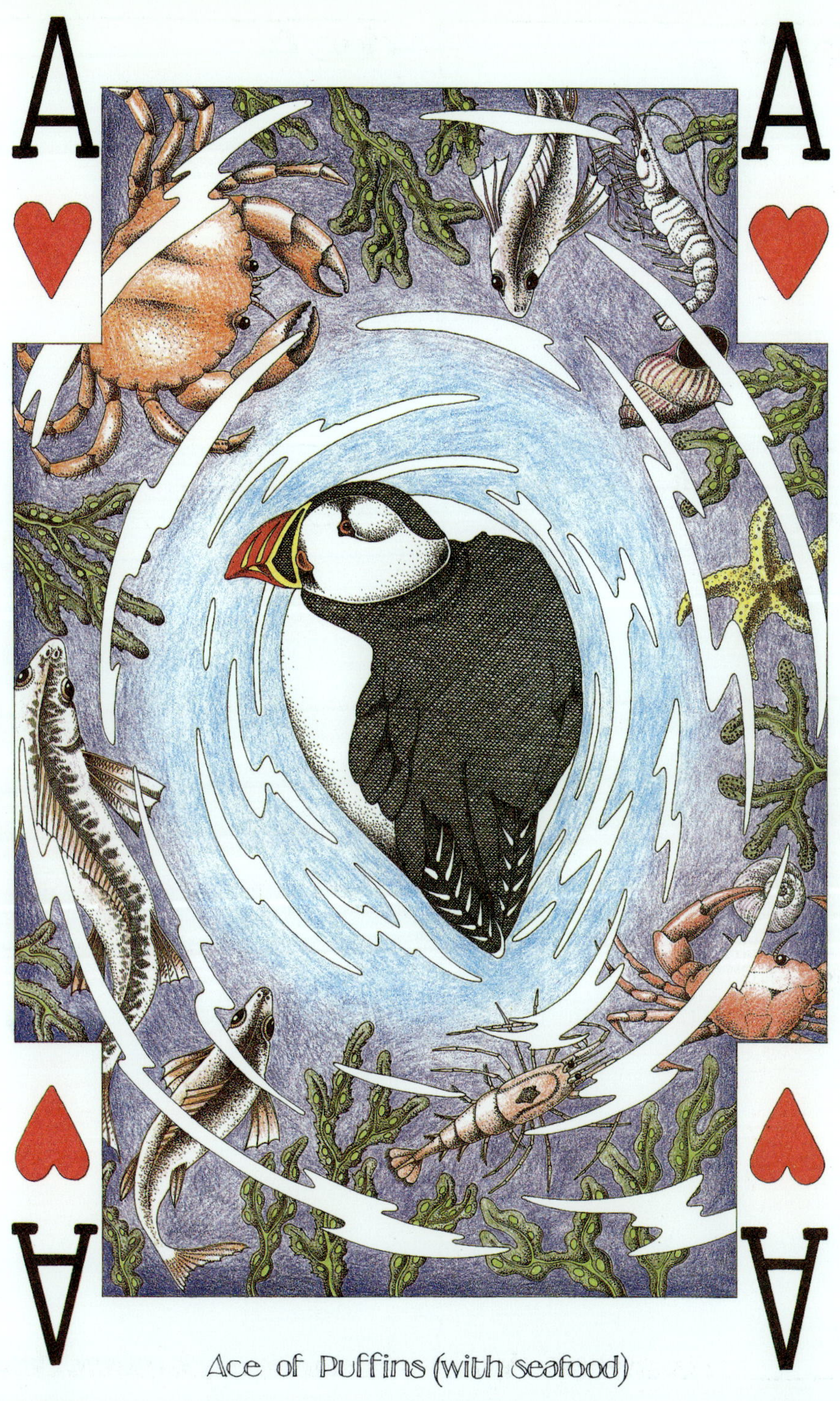

Ace of Puffins (with seafood)

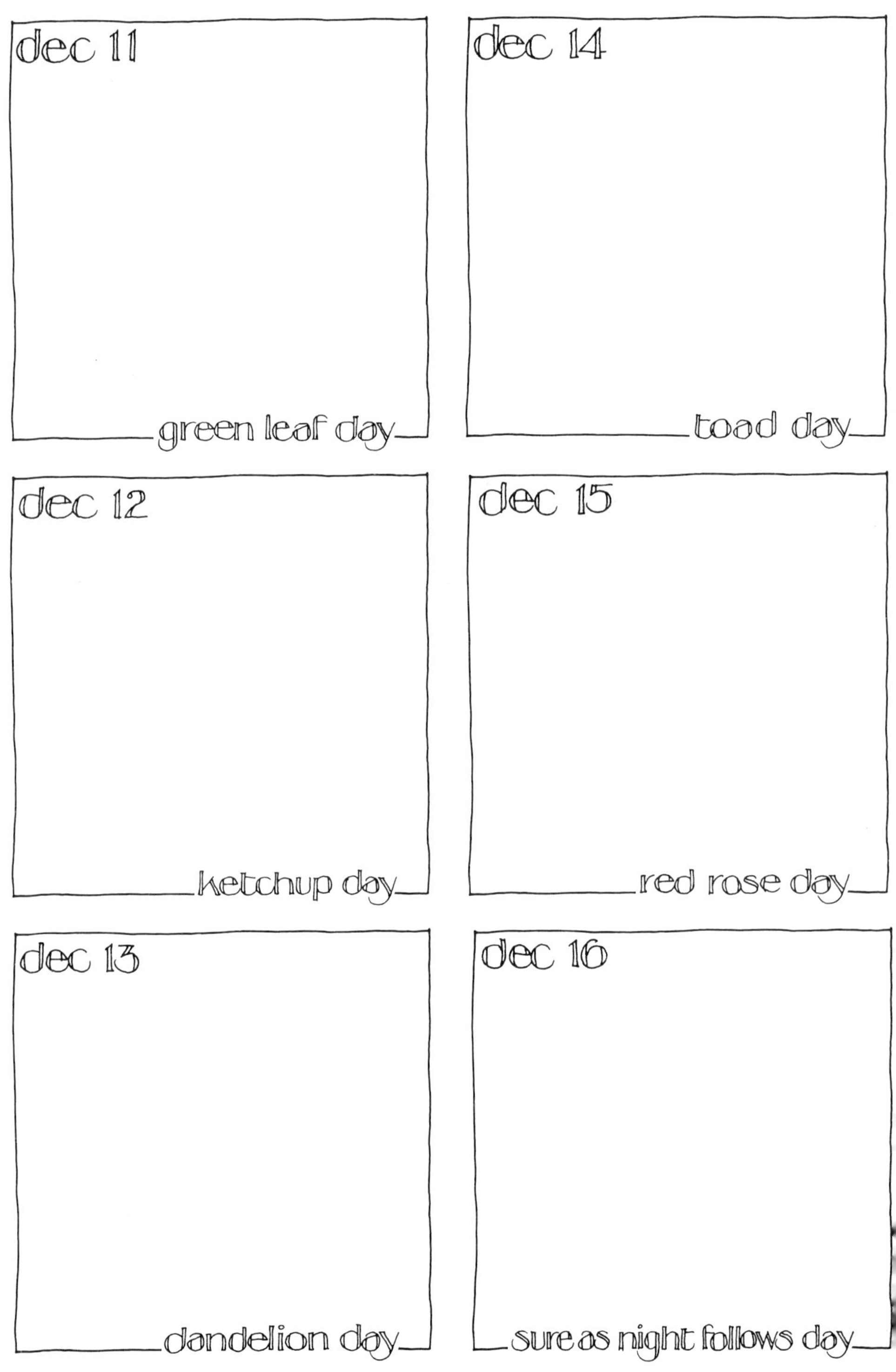

dec 11
green leaf day

dec 14
toad day

dec 12
ketchup day

dec 15
red rose day

dec 13
dandelion day

dec 16
sure as night follows day

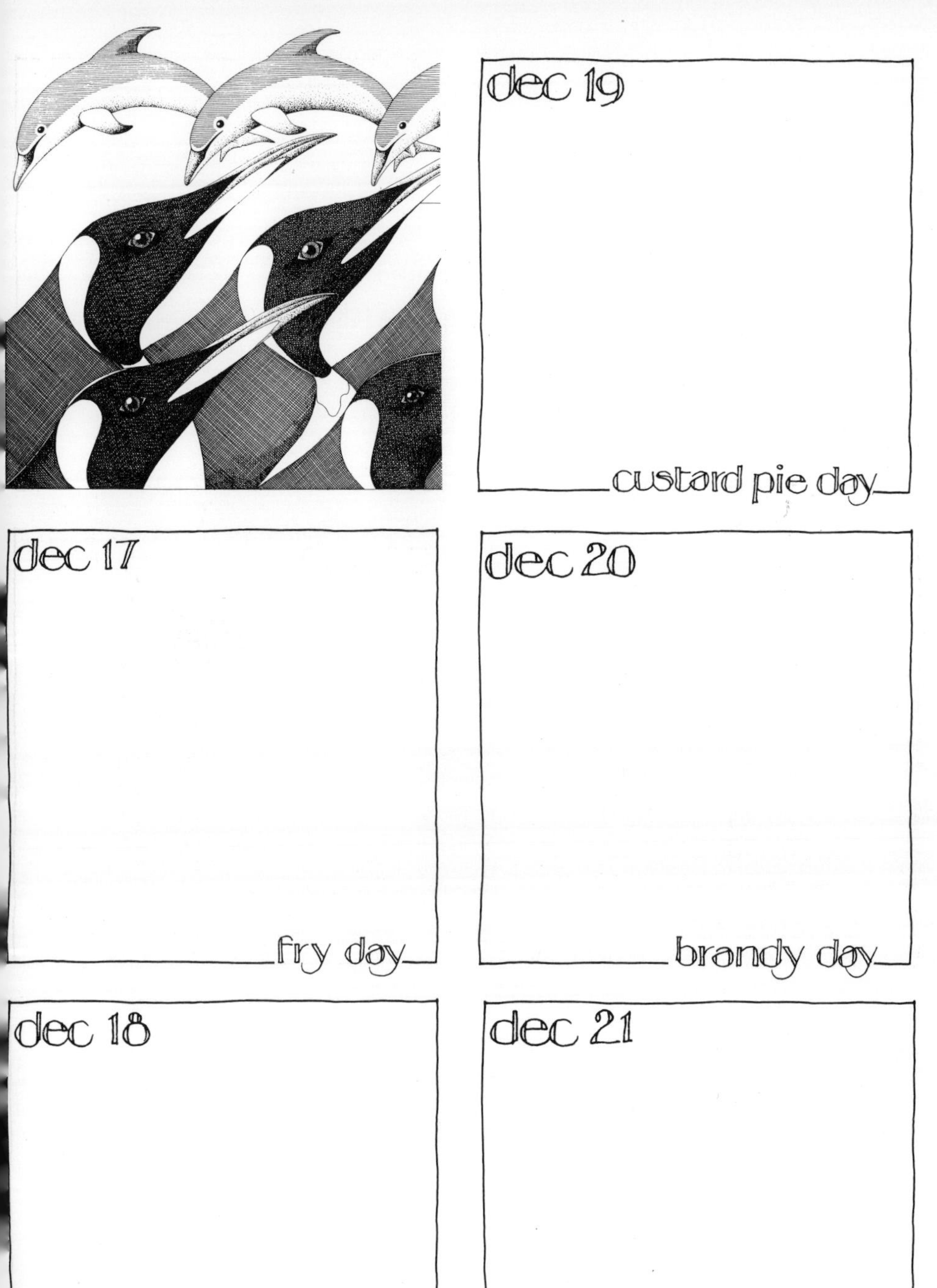

dec 17

fry day

dec 18

gingerbread day

dec 19

custard pie day

dec 20

brandy day

dec 21

raspberry day

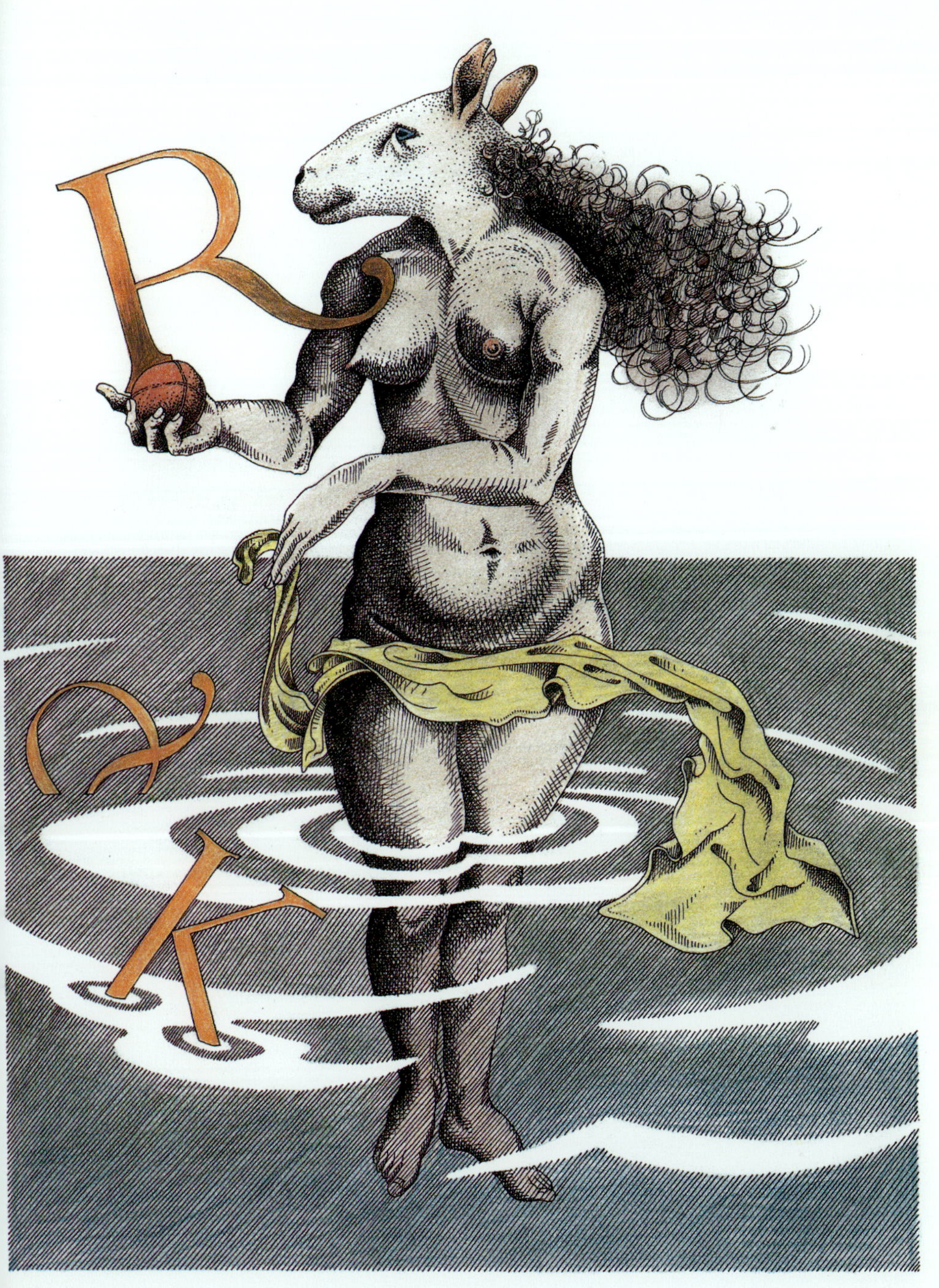

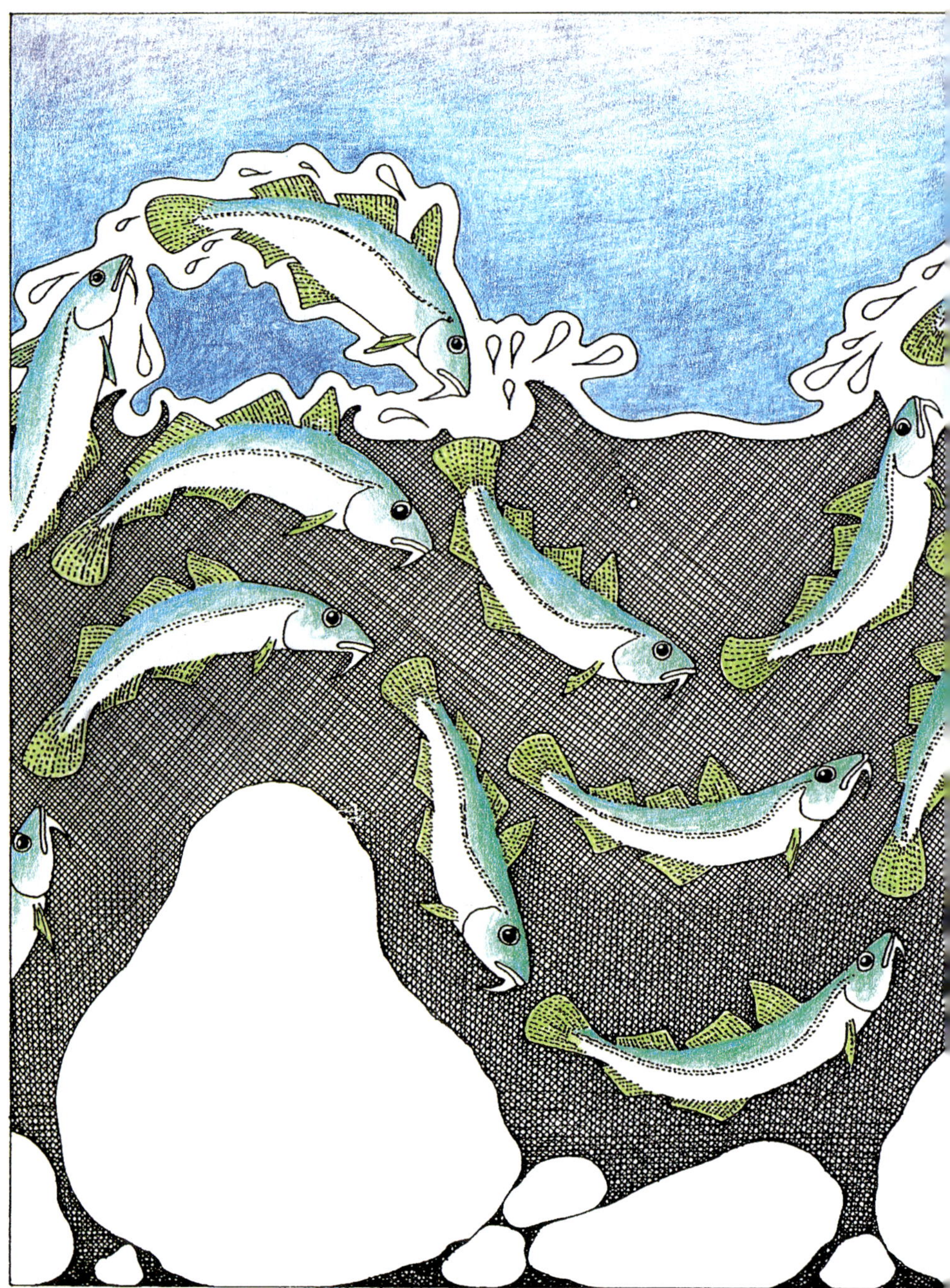